# *Powering Up*

## *LEARNING TO TEACH WELL*
## *WITH TECHNOLOGY*

# Powering Up

## LEARNING TO TEACH WELL
## WITH TECHNOLOGY

### Eileen M. Coppola

FOREWORD BY RICHARD F. ELMORE

TEACHERS
COLLEGE
PRESS

Teachers College, Columbia University
New York and London

Published by Teachers College Press, 1234 Amsterdam Avenue, New York, NY 10027

Copyright © 2004 by Teachers College, Columbia University

*Library of Congress Cataloging-in-Publication Data*

Coppola, Eileen M.
    Powering up : learning to teach well with technology / Eileen M. Coppola ; foreword by Richard F. Elmore.
      p.  cm.
    Includes bibliographical references (p.  ) and index.
    ISBN 0-8077-4499-9 (cloth : alk. paper) — ISBN 0-8077-4498-0 (pbk. : alk. paper)
    1. Computer-assisted instruction—Case studies.  2. Education—Curricula—Data processing—Case studies.  3. Educational technology—Case studies.  I.  Title.

  LB1028.5.C628  2004
  371.33'4—dc22                                        2004051650

ISBN 0-8077-4498-0 (paper)
ISBN 0-8077-4499-9 (cloth)

Printed on acid-free paper
Manufactured in the United States of America

11  10  09  08  07  06  05  04    8  7  6  5  4  3  2  1

*To Saleh, Amani, and Kiyan*

# Contents

**PART III**
**Teacher Learning and Organizational Culture: Implications**
**for Leadership and Policy** 105

# *Foreword*

LET ME BEGIN with a confession. When Eileen Coppola came to me with the idea of writing a dissertation on teachers' use of technology in a high school (a study that eventually become this book), I greeted it with—to be polite—mixed feelings. I knew Eileen to be a person of enormous insight and talent—a writer, a researcher, and an educational practitioner of the highest order; a person who exemplifies that blend of practical expertise and analytic skill we have tried hard to cultivate at the Harvard Graduate School of Education. I knew that if there were something to be learned from the study of technology in high schools, Eileen would find it.

On the other hand, my own experience suggested that there was, at best, little new to be learned. Hadn't Larry Cuban already said it? In the two years or so preceding Eileen's study, in my practice as a teacher, researcher, and consultant, I had visited dozens of schools that had made substantial investments in technology, and I had seen exactly one school where I could say there was any clear and visible increment to the learning of students attributable to technology. Mostly, my observations of "technology use" in schools were of students doing electronic worksheets, mining predigested databases for factoids that could be uncritically pasted into term papers, experimenting with font sizes and margins to increase the length of written assignments, and pushing against the boundaries of abject boredom by surreptitiously playing computer games in the absence of adult supervision. All this mindless activity was covered in a patina of cloying enthusiasm for the marvels of modern technology. An additional complication arose when I noticed that the most powerful instructional practice I was observing in my visits to schools typically involved technologies no more sophisticated than paper and pencil. An adaptation of an old analogy came to mind: Educational technology is to education as military music is to music. I found myself becoming a confirmed Luddite.

I did my best, first, to politely discourage Eileen from undertaking this study, and then, recognizing that I was overmatched by her determination (and she is a truly determined person), I feigned enthusiasm and support. What has emerged from Eileen's work is the best reason I can think of for why professors should not be allowed to dictate the subjects of students' dissertations. If professors were (improbably) required to pay tuition to their students for the new knowledge that students bring to them, then I would owe Eileen a substantial debt. She has been my teacher. And if she hasn't exactly eliminated my Luddite tendencies altogether, she has given us a powerful new way of understanding the meaning of technology in the practice of teaching.

At the core of Coppola's analysis is a deceptively simple, but powerful, idea: The use of technology for instructional purposes is a practice. This practice, as with all important practices, is socially constructed. It is a product of the values, knowledge, and skills of individuals. It is influenced in powerful ways by the social and cultural contexts in which it develops. It can be understood by close observation and analysis of practitioners. And that understanding can be turned into powerful normative ideas for the improvement and deepening of practice.

Closely connected to this core idea is the cognate, and equally powerful, idea that the effect of technology on students' access to knowledge is determined by the pedagogical knowledge and skill of teachers. Technology enables teachers with well-developed working theories of student learning to extend the reach and power of those theories; in the absence of these powerful theories, technology enables mediocrity.

Social practices are often aggravatingly indeterminate in the eyes of reformers looking for simple prescriptions. As Coppola says of the practices of the teachers she studied, "I found common predispositions and processes among the five, but no common techniques or prescriptions." The idea that instructional technologies lead to predictable changes in teaching practice—in the sense, say, that Henry Ford's assembly line led to predictable production processes—is not borne out by Coppola's study. In fact, to the degree that the effects of technology are determined by teachers' preexisting knowledge and skill, one would expect powerful uses of instructional technology to expand the variability of practice among highly knowledgeable teachers rather than reduce it.

Coppola is at some pains to point out that the connection between technology and teaching practice is a fundamentally rational one. Teachers make decisions about whether and how to use technology "based largely on their determination of the pedagogical value added by the technology." Differences among users, agnostics, and nonusers in her study are largely differences in degree rather than differences in kind. Users and agnostics are more persistent than nonusers in their attempts to understand the relationship between their working theories of instructional practice and technologies, not fundamentally different in their predisposition toward technology. To understand how technology connects to practice we must take seriously the knowledge and skill that teachers bring to the task of deciding what to teach and how. Coppola models what this process might look like with her own persistent questions: "How did you learn to do that? Why did you set up the activity in that way? Why did you handle that student's question the way you did? What were you thinking about? What will you do next? What do you think went well during this class? What didn't?"

Social practices are heavily influenced by the culture and structure of the organizations in which they operate. It becomes clear in Coppola's analysis exactly how this process works, and also how distinctive Woodland High School is in the culture that surrounds instructional practice. Moving from the problems of individual practice that stimulate and enable powerful uses of technology to the organizational processes that reinforce those uses requires seeing the work of administrators and leaders as enablers of powerful practice rather than as instruments of control. Since teachers' use of technology for powerful instructional purposes stems from their own understanding and ownership of a theory of instructional practice, leadership consists of enabling this understanding and ownership, rather than dictating particular practices.

Let me conclude with a few words about the place of this study in the literature on education reform more generally. The dominant view of serious students of educational reform about the relationship between technology and educational practice is probably closest to that of Larry Cuban, who is well known for arguing that technology, like most reforms du jour, tends to be co-opted into existing practices rather than exercising any transformative effect on practice. This view has had the effect of subjecting the overheated rhetoric of technology gurus to the cold analysis of enacted practice. Coppola does the field a service by taking Cuban's challenge frontally. Instead of arguing that technology does, in fact, exercise a powerful effect on instructional practice, she asks what conditions promote the connection of technology to practice, thereby shifting the terms of the debate from "whether" to "under what conditions."

People who specialize in applications of technology to education tend to be fascinated with their own gizmos. They are interested in getting teachers to "adopt" and "implement" particular instructional technologies that they believe will exercise a profoundly transformative effect on instructional practice and student learning. In this way, they become victims of their own rhetoric. By adopting this posture, they fall into the "implementation trap." That is, the results they promise depend on teachers' faithful implementation of the design specifications of their gizmos. We have known, with about as much certainty as it is possible to know anything in the social sciences, for at least

30 years that this is a bankrupt theory of educational improvement. The variability in practice and performance among teachers implementing a common model predictably exceeds the variability in practice and performance among competing models. Another way of saying this is that instructional models, no matter how well-designed, never dictate practice; individual knowledge and skill and organizational culture always trump externally initiated models. Yet the sponsors of technological innovations in education continue, with Sisyphian regularity, to urge adoption and implementation.

Coppola joins an alternative view of the relationship between technology and instructional practice, a view that might be characterized as "response theory." If all effects of externally initiated practices are mediated by individual and organizational factors, then the study of these practices should be conceived of as the study of individual and organizational responses, rather than the study of adoption, implementation, and fidelity. Although Coppola makes good use of traditional theories of innovation, her perspective is essentially subversive of these theories. If we were serious about the uses of technology in instructional practice, she argues, we would ground these studies in the instructional problems teachers have to solve (rather than the ones we wish they would solve) and we would study their responses to and uses of technology in the face of those problems, rather than the fidelity with which they implement our cherished gizmos.

Back now to my initial confession. Through this process of reading and responding to Eileen's work, the line between teacher and student has become hopelessly blurred—a sign that something called learning is occurring. And now I pass that privilege to a broader audience of readers.

Richard F. Elmore
*Gregory Anrig Professor of Educational Leadership*
*Harvard Graduate School of Education*

# Acknowledgments

I EXTEND my most sincere gratitude to the individuals and institutions who have supported this work. First and foremost, I wish to acknowledge the generosity of the principal, faculty, and former assistant superintendent for the school called Woodland High School in this book. My first contact with the school was facilitated by the assistant superintendent at that time. He was recommended by the National School Boards Association as a leader who had an exceptional vision for how to lead a school district in instructional technology. He opened every possible door for this research and was an astute guide throughout the process. Our many conversations demonstrated for me the complexity of leading instructional technology development, which meant for him having both vision and openness to the participation of others. He passed away suddenly in the summer of 1998 and is sorely missed by the Woodland community.

The principal of Woodland was equally welcoming and visionary. She provided broad access and support for a project that was relatively amorphous at first. She allowed open access to classrooms, suggested whom to see and where to look, and gave generously of her time during our several formal interviews and many conversations. The five teachers featured in this book's case studies welcomed me into their classrooms and their professional lives. Not only did they allow me to observe their teaching whenever I wished, but also they displayed incredible patience as I plied them with questions (some of which must have seemed batty) and followed them around on their daily routines. Their openness and intelligence constituted the fulcrum around which I was able to build the rest of the study. My thanks also extend to the other faculty and students at Woodland who generously participated and offered their guidance. It is truly an exceptional school.

This research was initially conducted as a dissertation study under the auspices of the Harvard Graduate School of Education (HGSE). Richard Elmore, my advisor, who early recommended that I "think hard about whether technology in and of itself can change teaching," helped push and prod me to pivotal insights at several points during the research. His thinking, his engagement with my arguments, and his encouragement of my scholarship have had a profound influence on this work. Martha Stone Wiske, also at HGSE, helped me to think in great detail about the relationships among strong pedagogy, technology, and school organization. She played a crucial role in pushing me toward more precision in my formulations and descriptions. Linda Wing, of the Urban Superintendents Program, offered her sharp mind throughout, reading many drafts with great attention. Her close consideration of my work and vision for the possibility of new technologies to support instruction contributed greatly to this finished product. My graduate school colleagues—Judy Pace, Ben Sanders, Antonia Rudenstine, and Elizabeth DeBray—as well as my sister and colleague, Barbara Coppola, read drafts, critiqued protocols and analyses, and offered many new ideas. Without such knowledgeable and supportive friends, intellectual work would be impossible.

I received generous financial support from various grants sponsored by the Harvard Graduate School of Education and the Urban Superintendents Program at HGSE, as well as funding from the Spencer Foundation in the form of a Research Training Grant. I wish to thank Bob Peterkin and Linda Wing of the Urban Superintendents Program for their commitment to the importance of serious research for the practice of leadership. Their commitment to linking research with practice strengthens the field.

I developed this book at the Center for Education at Rice University. The mentorship I have received from Linda McNeil, codirector of the center and a professor at Rice, is unparalleled. She thought this should be a book, and so it is. I am grateful for the financial and practical support offered by Linda and Ron Sass (the other codirector of the center), the phenomenal editorial support of Laurie Hammons, and the generous practical support of Debra Gamble, Catherine Crawford, and Glenda White, all staff at the Center for Education. In addition I want to thank Brian Ellerbeck, Acquisitions Editor at Teachers College Press, for his support throughout the publishing process.

My deepest personal gratitude goes to my husband, Saleh Fawaz, and my two daughters, Amani and Kiyan. Saleh has always had the remarkable quality of supporting my work in as many ways as it takes, and there have certainly been very many ways over the years. My sister-in-law Judy Coppola and her mother, our adopted nana Dee Kanachovski, helped me to balance the demands of work and motherhood at some critical moments since I became a parent. Inevitably, it is the patience and love of family that carries the day.

# Introduction

ON A VISIT to an inner-city high school in the mid-1990s, I conversed with a technology teacher as she surveyed a room full of brand-new, cutting-edge computers. She spoke about how she was teaching a computer applications course by collaborating with an English teacher, so that her students would experience interesting, important content at the same time as they learned word processing and desktop publishing. As our conversation deepened, she described her dream of integrating these computers throughout the curriculum, but admitted she was struggling with how to do it. She motioned to all the new hardware and declared: "So much power, and not a clue how to use it."

New technologies certainly seem to hold bright promise for education. Computers, in particular, are so shiny, so fast, and can do such amazing things that the possibilities seem truly awesome. But what exactly can we do with computers in schools? And how? And will what we do be better than what came before?

This book makes a spare and simple argument: Developing high-quality uses of computers in schools depends on keeping high-quality teaching at the core of the school. Only when sound pedagogical ideas are at the center of a school's culture, when they drive the hundreds—or thousands—of decisions made by educators on a daily basis, can they foster intelligent, high-quality uses of new technologies. The success of the school in this regard lies in its ability to keep its most important ideas central and put technology at the service of those ideas.

## PARADOX: THE PROMISE AND PERILS OF NEW TECHNOLOGIES

It has always seemed apparent to me that computer technology held the promise to enhance education. First of all, it simplifies a great many rote tasks, allowing its users to focus on other, presumably more advanced, aspects of their work. This should be good for education because it means students and their teachers can focus on what Benjamin Bloom would call "higher order thinking skills," such as analysis and synthesis (Bloom, 1956).

For example, computers, through word processing, make the laborious task of writing prose a much faster one. Instead of having to write out the final draft of a school assignment, students can edit and print. Instead of spending time copying over sections that are already fine, they can spend their time editing the sections that are not. Word processing and networking simplify sharing drafts through local servers, e-mail, text-markup, and version-tracking facilities. The time saved allows teachers and learners to focus on the heart of the matter: developing voice, tone, form, content, style, organization, flow, power, argument, character, plot, or other vital elements of writing.

With a simple spreadsheet, a student can create a matrix of data from which to build graphs and charts. Using this technology, students can practice categorizing data, putting it into readable tables, and developing algebraic formulas for key calculations. They can manipulate the data quickly and easily to try a variety of different graphical formats for presenting it. The setup is perfect for lessons on whether to use a line, pie, or bar graph; how many sets of data to put on one chart; or how to find the right scale to make a particular point. Spreadsheets can anchor a data set shared among class members or between classes, facilitating conversations about how to analyze—or create models for—the same data. The time saved by automating and sharing data, and by quickly producing charts, gives teachers and students more time to spend understanding the patterns of that data, hypothesizing their meaning, and experimenting with displays that help an analyst understand trends and express them to others.

Other software applications can enhance teaching in specific subject areas. Statistics courses are vastly different now that standard deviations, coefficients, and $p$-values can be calculated by computers. With time saved on calculations, teachers and students can spend more time mastering statistical concepts, understanding what the statistics tell them and what they do not, and learning the many tools available to analyze naturally occurring numerical data.

The Internet provides access to a truly incredible field of information. It clearly saves time for students doing research and offers access to a far wider range of resources than a school or local library. Students can now easily access a wide variety of periodical indexes and online articles. Searches for relevant books are more efficient and more accurate when done via online catalogs, and searches can also be conducted at remote libraries for interlibrary loans. The primary sources available on the Web are astounding: genomic, geological, and chemical databases; genealogical and demographic data; photographic and visual art libraries; music downloads; and Library of Congress historical documents are just a few examples. Students can read articles from newspapers in other states or other nations, search official Web sites, or locate commentary on the same topic from differing perspectives. The process of moving from link to link in exploration is itself a fascinating demonstration of the interconnectedness of knowledge.

When students build Web sites themselves, they have the opportunity to create multidimensional representations of knowledge. They can define branches that lead to other branches and to information outside the site, which may circle back around again. Their Web sites can embody some of the categories, layers, and interrelationships of a topic. Organizing information into a Web site requires the complex cognitive tasks of classifying, interrelating, and expressing knowledge. If approached with a sense of academic rigor, Web page or Web site production requires students to categorize information and cross-reference it, at the very least. It requires them to create a core document with links to relevant resources. To take full advantage of the possibilities of webmastering, teachers can insist that students create a presentation that includes a theory for how to present information on a particular topic, then insist that the Web site be a coherent representation of a web of knowledge.

Subject-specific software may also be valuable for teaching when it is well designed or when it is used as a professional tool. Engineering, architectural, CAD-CAM, publishing, graphics, or animation software are just a few examples. Well-designed educational software, if also well used, can make a valuable addition to classroom teaching. Some of the best packages create structured environments for exploration. Computer-based simulations allow for a complex group of variables to interact so that students can experience— and manipulate—social science, natural science, or mathematical phenomena even with limited resources. Simulations like these allow teachers to target concept development and analytical skills through controlled environments designed for teaching specific ideas. Others, such as the CSILE system developed at the University of Toronto (2003) and now marketed as *Knowledge Forum,* set up an environment for communication that structures learning experiences in order to take advantage of multiple sources of expertise (Scardamalia, Bereiter, Brett, et al., 1992; Scardamalia, Bereiter, & Lamon, 1994; Scardamalia, Bereiter, McLean, Swallow, & Woodruff, 1991–92). As the technology advances, an ever wider range of simulations are becoming available.

These are but a few examples of possible uses of computers for teaching, but a shift to a more critical stance generates some important pedagogical questions: Will word processing change the way students learn to write? Will they write so quickly that they don't think carefully first? If students analyze data using computer software, will they ever learn to create their own data matrices and graphs? How will they understand how graphs and charts are made if they can simply push a few buttons? When will students ever read a book? Isn't the information on the Internet too shallow? How do we teach them to gauge the reliability of what they find on the Internet? What about plagiarism? Won't students just cut and paste from the Web? Aren't simulations just like games? What content will students learn from them? Will they come to think that all learning has to be "fun," like a video game?

Based on the research described in this book, I believe the answers to these questions boil down to a simple proposition: Whether computers are used well depends on the pedagogical knowledge and skill of the teachers who design their use in the classroom. While it is possible to use computers in the powerful ways I've described, it is also possible to use them in ways that waste time or are actually detrimental to learning. Students may present very professional-looking papers or graphs without having learned much of anything about writing or data analysis. They can use a powerful search engine to find sites on the Internet, such that reading a couple of screens at each site becomes all there is to research. They can fiddle so long with the animation on a PowerPoint presentation that they only learn superficially the content they are supposed to present. Is it any wonder that there are skeptics when it comes to the value of computers for classroom teaching?

## Technology Integration: A View from the Classroom

My own experiences as a teacher in technology-poor and technology-rich schools and as a technology integration specialist in a public school constitute the basis for the questions I explored in this research. Where I began my teaching career—in an inner-city middle school with minimal technology—computers were used mostly as babysitters, with the exception of some computer applications classes. In the early 1990s, only a limited number of computers were available to this poorly resourced school, so their integration into daily instruction was not even a real possibility. Resource and structural barriers had to be overcome before the more complex issue of instructional integration could be tackled.

I later moved to a second school, a combined middle and high school, where technology was a central element and, according to the school's rhetoric, was supposed to be integrated throughout the curriculum. It was there, I thought, in a school with relatively high access and expertise, that ideas about using computers for teaching could really be tested. But even within my own teaching, a humanities course that combined English and history, I found this technology integration a great challenge. First, using computers required that I work through the politics of access. How much access could I get for my students? Daily? Weekly? How many computers could we get to use at once? If every student could have a computer available at all times, we could begin to integrate them as a daily tool, mirroring the way adults use them, but this was not the case. So, after I had gained access, I had to figure out how to fit the form of that access with a curriculum and a series of lessons.

I decided that having the computers available to my students for the period of a unit or project would yield deeper learning possibilities than a once-a-week pattern. I was able to schedule my class in a computer lab for a period of several weeks. This approximated what I wanted, but at the same time it set up expectations in the students that they would be able to use the computers constantly during class time. That, of course, would make little sense, since we had content to learn that would require reading, lecture, discussion, and research. The computer lab, however, was set up so there was little other space for students to work except seated at the computers. My solution at those times was to turn the computers off, but since the students were so eager to use them, tension was always in the air about when they would be turned on again.

I had a more ideal situation later in the year when my class had access to computers (about a 4:1 ratio) in the library, where I was also able to teach my class. During that semester, we began to use the computers more fluidly: On some days, all students used them; on other days, they used them as needed; on still other days, they remained idle. I saw the importance then of having enough machines in the classroom for everyone to use (even if not one machine for each student), but positioning them so that they were tools on the side, such that they left room for other work as well. Computers should not be located only in labs, but also in regular classrooms, accessible and organized, like tools you pick up when you need them. When I or my colleagues had to adjust to any other arrangement, such as having only one or two computers in a classroom or working sporadically in a computer lab, we had to adjust the instruction to fit our access to technology, instead of using the technology to fit our conception of instruction.

Here's an example of how this would work. Let's say we had 30 seventh- and eighth-grade students in a class with 12 computers. Of course, we first needed to ensure that every student was acquainted with basic computer operations and software use. For everyone to learn to operate the machines, however, time on them was required for each individual student, because if everyone sat at the machines for a group lesson, some students inevitably tuned out while others operated the mouse and keyboard. Another option was to split the class, teaching one group on the computers and having the rest work quietly, then switching at the next class session. This worked to some extent, provided the group off the computers needed little or no help and little or no discipline, which was unlikely. Another problem was that for 30 students with 12 computers, three such sessions were necessary in order to give every student individual time at the keyboard. Over time, however, our students became acquainted with basic hardware and software operation so that the initial problems diminished.

When we got down to the work of the curriculum, two or three children had to use each computer, so group work was in order. This meant helping our students develop the ability to work together and share the computer. Too often one student would develop into the "mouser" while others hung back. Usually, it was up to the teacher to develop a system for sharing and rotating.

What I'm describing has been well documented by research as the teacher's challenge of shifting classroom management and culture to suit the dynamics of computer use by students. In some cases, this shift may be a positive one toward a more student-centered practice, but in other cases, the structure of computer access can come to dominate the choices a teacher is able to make regarding instruction and student routines. (See, for example, David, 1990; Means, 1991; Newman, 1991; Sandholtz, Ringstaff, & Dwyer, 1997; Trumbull, 1989; Wiske & Houde, 1993.)

In my own journey, I next faced the challenge of developing instruction around available hardware and software. Often teachers are presented with the resources available and asked to integrate technology. Instead of being allowed to choose software, teachers are too often provided with software chosen by a district or building administrator. This means adapting one's instruction to the available software packages, when really a teacher should choose software and hardware as tools to bolster the instruction. In our case, we were simply given the hardware and software to use in any given year. Sometimes in the spring we were presented with a small software budget to use for the next year, but unfortunately, the budgeting process usually required decisions within a few days, without the benefit of knowing what courses we would be teaching the next year. Under those conditions, choosing specific software packages that would actually be useful was rather unlikely.

Once access and software were secured and a unit was planned, we jumped into the fray of the classroom, and we hoped day to day that all the computers would work. If software behaved unexpectedly, a computer crashed, or a network went down, a whole lesson plan could go by the wayside. Most days there were just little things: students losing work, a computer freezing up. Of course, it was best to work on the newer computers if possible. One day, I had a 90-minute class in the late afternoon. The students were developing Civil War newspapers—not a terribly original assignment, but one that required research, writing, and some attempt to enter the mind-set of a person living in a Union or Confederate state. I had signed up for the computer lab so the students could use the word processors for developing their papers. Twenty minutes into the class period, the computer network crashed. It froze completely. Nothing we did could revive it. I was left with 27 eighth graders with 70 minutes until the end of the school day and no backup lesson. We had some books available for research, but most students had already completed their research and were ready to write and design their newspapers. Some hunkered down and wrote longhand, but it was a fairly challenging hour for all. I learned then what all experienced computer-using teachers know: If you are using technology, you need a backup plan.

This story illustrates why integrating computers at a deep level can be overwhelming without a structure and culture at the school that provides support from many different angles. Essential components for success include being able to plan in advance by knowing what you will teach, having access to troubleshooting support during classes, and having access to the computers as driven by instructional needs. Without these, genuine integration is extremely difficult, perhaps impossible. I should say that administrators at this school, almost a decade ago, tried to establish good conditions for teaching with technology. At that time we were all learning, and we are learning still.

In my second year at this same school, I was assigned the role of coteacher with a number of colleagues who wished to integrate technology into their work but needed support. I proposed this coteaching model, with the idea that two of us would work side by side to develop technology uses that made sense for the required teaching and curriculum. As long as we were able to meet to plan the classes, this generally worked well. But another surprise was in store for me. One science teacher had very specific ideas about how he wished to use computers to support his pedagogical approach. He wanted me to create for him a notebook system so that students could transfer an outline from the textbook chapter to a word processor, then fill in summary notes within each section. This could not have been further from my vision of how computers should support constructivist teaching. I tried to explore other options with him, demonstrating a videodisc (which we used at that time) with science content and how databases and spreadsheets could be used to analyze data. He would not have any of it, firm in his conviction that his students would best learn science by outlining the textbook.

It has sometimes been proposed that computers could change teaching toward a more constructivist, collaborative approach (Becker, 2000; Becker & Riel, 1999; Cohen, 1987; Cuban, 1986, 2001; David, 1990; Means &

Olson, 1995; Sandholtz et al., 1997; Sheingold, 1990; Sheingold & Tucker, 1990; Trumbull, 1989; Wiske & Houde, 1993). However, this science-teacher incident demonstrated to me that the computers themselves had no magical powers and could be used as tools for rote learning as well as for higher level thinking.

## Technology Integration: Views from the School and the District

My continued involvement at the school and district levels provided many further examples of the many pitfalls possible when schools attempt to use computers for constructivist or student-centered teaching. Too often the drive to use technology outweighed a school's ability to produce high-quality instructional experiences with technology.

Integrating computers into school life is a high-stakes enterprise. The machines themselves are, of course, costly. The U.S. Bureau of the Census (2002) reports that in 2000–01 there was an average of one computer for every 4.4 public school students in the United States, and that public school enrollment was 47.8 million. That means U.S. public schools housed approximately 10.8 million computers at that time. Anderson and Becker (2001) estimate that total technology expenditures in fiscal year 1998 were approximately 2.7% of total educational expenditures for that year. They report that "the average school spends $114 per year per student on technology, with only $22.50 of that for teacher support services, about $8 for software, and the remainder for hardware" (p. 5). It is easy to argue that this is not enough funding or that it is distributed wrongly, but even expending a basic level of resources creates a drive to make good use of the computers, a drive that combines with the gee-whiz nature of new technologies in a way that can supersede pedagogical considerations.

As my work branched out to include leadership on the school and district levels, I found that almost everyone thought it was extremely important to have cutting-edge technology in schools. The arguments generally ran along these lines:

1. Students need to learn computer skills to prepare them for an increasingly computerized workplace.
2. Computers can make learning more efficient by doing the teaching for teachers.
3. Computers symbolize progress and modernity, which is important for schools as they compete in an increasingly privatized market for education, and important for school districts wanting to attract middle- and high-income residents to their districts.
4. Computers can lead to higher achievement and higher motivation.

These arguments—which are debatable—represent various facets of the pervasive but mostly tacit assumption that it is naturally good to have computers in schools.

Researchers as well as educational administrators engage in this assumption. Practitioners and researchers in the field of *technology integration*, as it is commonly called, share the opinion that technology is good for schools, that it strengthens instruction, and that teachers should be urged, or even mandated, to use it. This assumption is central to the field and has come to drive most discussions of research and practice. A corollary assumption is that teachers who don't attempt to integrate technology are resistant to change, uninterested in new instructional techniques, or unwilling to do the hard work it takes to use classroom technology. In the technology integration field, there is a strong underlying norm that schools should be moving toward more technology use.

When the drive to get technology into instruction is too strong, I have observed that several types of results frustrate the successful marriage of quality teaching to new technologies. I call these types *cosmetic use*, the *technological imperative, romantic visions*, and the *dominance of politics*.

*Cosmetic use* occurs when schools and teachers feel they must look like they are using technology, so they develop the physical infrastructure and create lessons where students sit at computers, even though there may be little or no actual instructional value in the work. Schools may develop whole networks, labs, and classroom computers that they seldom use, except a few teachers and students in a few class sessions. Schools and districts often expend significant resources on hardware and software, only to use them in limited and superficial ways. The pressures on faculty may be sufficiently strong that teachers will make sure their students are sitting in front of the computers, even though the software they are using may be of questionable value, or their use of the Internet merely involves superficial Web surfing on trivial topics. Sitting students at computers and assigning them tasks is much easier than developing technology uses that facilitate teaching and learning.

This type of computer use often occurs when administrators mandate technological configurations from the top, an illustration of how well-intended policy mandates do not automatically translate into good practice. For example, requiring that all computers be placed one or two per classroom, or that all computers be placed in labs is a common strategy pursued by administrators who want to promote their use schoolwide or districtwide. Often, they are themselves under pressure from more senior administrators, school board members, or a granting agency to make sure computers are used in teaching. In fact, neither the placement of the machines nor their use can be successfully mandated from the top. Teachers need to decide for themselves how computers should be placed, so that they can use them in ways that make sense given the flow of instruction.

I have also seen schools driven by the *technological imperative*, where computer use is driven by the technology rather than the curriculum. When telecommunications technologies advance, it becomes the thing to use. As desktop computers become more capable of high resolution graphics, it in turn seems vital to incorporate these. Conversations among adults working to employ the technological imperative tend to orient around new finds of trendy, cutting-edge hardware or software. The implication is that since it's new—and often amazing—it should be incorporated into schools because whatever is new is good, regardless of its educational value.

This was clearly the case when the Internet became more easily accessible through advances in desktop graphic capabilities combined with the e-rate discount for schools and libraries during the 1990s. It seemed like a good idea for students to use the Internet, and teachers felt pressured to do so by administration, parents, and students. But how beneficial is it to use the Internet for research if students' work is neither structured around specific learning goals nor embedded in an overall curriculum? There are important questions that should be answered before even trying to incorporate the Internet: What does it add to existing ways of doing research? What are its advantages and disadvantages? What should we teach children about what the Internet is, when its information is valuable, and when it is not?

Another example is when teachers decide to have students do Power-Point or HTML presentations because the product looks so polished, then quickly find out that learning the software and adding bells and whistles take an enormous amount of class time away from teaching the subject. This can result in nice-looking presentations on which students have spent a lot of time, but which contain little academic content. Finally mindless use also occurs when administrators or teachers adopt software programs without really analyzing their worth and think that if students are looking at a computer screen and operating a keyboard they must be learning.

*Romantic visions* drive technology use when leaders entertain abstract, romantic notions of its possibilities. Some people believe computers can replace teachers, be more efficient than teachers, increase class size, decrease cost, and motivate students. I have always wondered how this would be possible. For example, a scientist friend who served on his local school board argued that by investing in computer technology, schools would be more efficient because technology had made business more efficient. This is a weak analogy, because children are much more complex as "raw material" than plastics or metal. At another time, a representative from an education ministry in South America approached me to ask whether installing computers in schools throughout the country would enable them to increase their class size from 40 to 70. The idea behind this was that the computers would do what no teacher could: motivate and guide the learning of 70 young individuals in a single classroom. Another common notion is that all education will someday occur online. Why would we want this to happen? Online education is certainly a valuable tool, and quality online courses can be powerful learning experiences. However, interpersonal and group interaction have some irreplaceable benefits for learning.

Finally, the *dominance of politics* may cause harmful conflict over technology. When access to computers is a struggle, the internal politics of the school comes into play as faculty compete for scarce resources. Since computers are expensive and computer use is valued in schools, gaining access to the computers can easily become a source of competition and micropolitical conflict. Where computer use is highly valued by the administration, those who do it well gain status in the organization; others may resent that status, and thus conflict among faculty arises. Subgroups of users versus nonuses often form, contributing an intergroup dynamic laced with competing values and assumptions. These dynamics may at times drain energy from the primary task of the school: to develop high-quality instruction that leads to powerful learning for children.

The question, then, is not simply whether computers are being used in classrooms, but how they are being used, and to what ends. In my experience, pursuit of cosmetic use, the technological imperative, romantic visions, or the domination of politics often consume time, energy, and resources with few or no instructional results. These phrases capture some of the typical struggles I have observed in schools when the push to use technology overtakes insistence on quality, when computer use itself seems a more important or more attainable goal than the quality of that use.

## RESEARCHING SUCCESS: A NATURAL EXPERIMENT

Out of these experiences, I began to wonder how a public school without large-scale grants or partnerships could accomplish not merely *use* of new technologies, but *quality use*. In a positive case, how did teachers learn to use computers as tools for constructivist teaching strategies? When this learning was successful, what organizational conditions supported their learning and facilitated their ability to use the technologies?

I sought to answer these questions through research. I wanted what ethnographers would call a "natural" setting where I could observe the successful practice I knew so many educators seek in their schools. I searched for a public high school that used technology throughout the school, along constructivist lines, and that was neither the recipient of a major grant for technology nor was partnered with a university-based design and research team.

This volume explores in detail how such a school successfully promoted quality uses of computers for constructivist teaching. In a yearlong ethnographic study, I examined the learning of five computer-using teachers in various core subject areas, explored how they learned to use computers, and analyzed what elements of the school's structure, organizational culture, and policy supported them. As I worked on the study, I realized that this research about technology held implications for other sorts of professional learning as well since many of the conditions necessary for constructivist teaching with technology also were necessary for teachers learning other new practices.

As it developed, the study became a journey not only into the world of classroom technology, but also into the world of standards, learning organizations, teacher learning, policy incentives, organizational structure, and normative and intellectual culture. In the end, it is no surprise that the study contains lessons for schools trying to improve instructional practice. The instance of learning to use technology for constructivist teaching is merely a case therein.

# PART I

# Computers, Pedagogy, and School Reform: Relationships and Intersections

THE STUDY of a whole school organization and how it learns to use computers for instruction requires a holistic approach, framed by theories from a wide range of perspectives. When the point is improvement and the topic is schools, a fully interdisciplinary perspective requires that researchers begin from the actuality of schooling and extend their analysis to include valuable ways of thinking about the problem. If the question is how teachers learn powerful new instructional practices, then we must consider such factors as the teachers themselves, their backgrounds and educational histories, and how they learn in the workplace. We must catalog and analyze the demands and supports emanating from the policy environments and the structures of the school, such as time, student load, course preparation, and grouping. And finally, we must do the difficult job of unearthing the tacit cultural norms and reigning ideas of the school—which turns out to be the most interesting task of all. To define the contours of this analysis, Chapters 1 and 2 introduce various ways of understanding aspects of the school environment that may either nurture or starve teachers' capacity to teach well with new technologies.

# High Technology, High Standards, and Cognitive Research: How Can Schools Meet Their Promise?

As COMPUTERS increasingly become part of daily life in our workplaces and our homes, it becomes more important than ever that we use them well in schools. Educators and policymakers widely agree that new technologies should be employed in ways that will mimic real-world uses in order to prepare students for the workplace or higher education. Some envision schools where computers will become everyday objects like pencils, books, or chalkboards, simply another tool for students and teachers. But despite many compelling visions, the presence of computers in schools continues to be limited; and even where the physical machines are accessible, they are too often used in ways that fail to take advantage of their potential (Becker, 1994, 2000; Becker, Ravitz, & Wong, 1999; Becker & Riel, 1999).

At the same time, our nation is increasingly concerned with education: politicians, policymakers, intellectuals, and field educators advocate higher level learning, stronger standards, and new instructional techniques based on recent research from cognitive science. Policy and leadership initiatives throughout the country are intended to create higher quality learning for an ever-expanding range of students. The issue of computer use is a problem embedded within the larger question of how to work to improve that instruction.

Here I examine the administrative, policy, and leadership issues of how structure and organizational culture influence improvement of the core practice of classroom teaching, paying particular attention to the use of computers for constructivist teaching as an important example—or case—of this broader challenge.

## THE VISION: COMPUTERS, NEW PEDAGOGIES, HIGH STANDARDS

"High-quality teachers," "technology," "new teaching methods," "high standards for all children"—citizens, educators, politicians, business leaders, and community leaders use these phrases to describe what they want from school. It seems everyone wants schools where the teachers excel; computers abound; the teaching is interesting, relevant, and powerful; and the learning is lifelong. How do we get there?

Since microcomputers became widely available in the early 1980s, educators and technologists have attempted to define what role they might play in teaching and learning. For some scholars and practitioners, it became apparent that using computers for constructivist pedagogy could be an important way to improve teaching. However, they found that adding computers to the classroom mix usually required new approaches to grouping, time, or curriculum at the school. Out of this discovery, some scholars proceeded to study the intersection of technology use and school restructuring. This work paralleled, but rarely crossed, the more general strand of research on restructuring schools, which was more nuanced on the elements and processes of school change but usually ignored the presence or absence of technology. The main findings and ideas from these three research strands: technology in education, constructivist teaching with computers, and school reform or restructuring provide an essential backdrop for this study.

### A Short History of Computers in Schools

The cry to introduce computers into classrooms "to prepare students for the 21st century," is a popular one. Business leaders, economists, and leaders in educational policy call for graduates who will be able to use computer and information technology as tools in higher education and employment. In the education press and the popular media, it is reported often and forcefully how important it is to get more computers into schools. This is generally assumed to be a good thing: Young people must know how to use computers to survive in "the information age" or "the 21st century." In his State of the Union address for 1999, President Clinton set high standards for the nation: "In our schools, every classroom in America must be connected to the information superhighway, with computers and good software, and well-trained teachers." Vice President Al Gore took the trouble to address the International Conference on Technology and Education that same year. The No Child Left Behind Act promoted by President Bush, and passed by Congress in 2001, "charges the Secretary of Education with developing the nation's third National Education Technology Plan. The Plan will establish a national strategy supporting the effective use of technology to improve student academic achievement and prepare them for the 21st century" (U.S. Department of Education, 2004). It is difficult to imagine in these times a school board or political candidate who would not, somewhere in his or her platform, support more computers in schools.

As a result, schools, districts, and states are spending millions of dollars on computer technology. To what effect? Few studies have been able to correlate achievement outcomes with technology use. Buying and maintaining the machines is an expensive prospect, as is training for teachers in using these new machines. Although the push for more computers in schools is virtually universal, in truth we have a limited capacity to use the machines well in classrooms, and bringing them into schools adds to educational costs already considered too great.

Two major government reports provide the early history of microcomputers in public schools. The first, called *Power On!* and published in 1988 by the federal Office of Technology Assessment (OTA), found that during the 1980s schools rapidly acquired computer hardware. In 1983 the national average was approximately one computer per 100 students, but by 1988 it was one computer per 30 students (U.S. Congress, 1988, p. 7), with 95% of those computers regularly used (p. 34). The report called for increased purchase of and access to hardware, citing lack of funding for computer purchases as the main barrier to increased use.

The second report, published by OTA in 1995, painted a different picture. More hardware was available in schools, but teachers were having trouble using it. The report projected that by the spring of that year, there would be one computer for every nine students, but that, "despite technologies available in schools, a substantial number of teachers report little or no use of computers for instruction" (U.S. Congress, 1995, p. 10). Authors of the 1995 OTA report recommended increased time for teacher learning, ongoing support, the development of better visions and rationales for using computers, and more focused assessments of learning outcomes. Additionally, they recommended increased funding for professional development at 30% of existing technology resources, while most districts at that time spent only 15%.

The results of this early research can be summarized as follows:

- Access to computers, while still too limited, has increased considerably over the almost 2 decades since it was originally chronicled.
- A significant proportion of teachers do not use computers at all, and very few employ them regularly.
- Teacher learning has been widely identified as a major barrier to wider computer use.

- Policymakers are beginning to recognize that teachers' knowledge-enabling use of these tools has not kept pace with hardware acquisition.
- Our notions of how to employ these tools have changed quickly, creating a rapidly changing environment and a significant challenge for schools and teachers.

Research on microcomputer use in schools also illustrates a history of shifts in what educators thought children should learn about computers and how they thought about computers in the context of their work (Becker, 1994; U.S. Congress, 1995). When educators first placed computers in classrooms in the early 1980s, many teachers and designers of instructional technology believed that the technology itself would alter the nature of instruction and the culture of the classroom. Technological and educational visionaries imagined that the presence of the microcomputer in the classroom would change the way teachers taught, the way students learned, and the way schools were organized. Software designers imagined that their vision of education would so pervade computer-using classrooms that traditional instructional approaches would be overtaken by the approach embedded within the software design (e.g., Papert, 1980; Snyder & Palmer, 1986).

Much early research on using computers in classrooms is striking for its failure to consider teachers as active agents in children's learning with computers. It was thought that well-designed software could create learning experiences for children that would foster high-level thinking skills. Children, computers, cognitive scientists, and instructional designers are present in this literature; teachers are absent. This was a strong and powerful perspective, one that is still prevalent among many software developers as well as in research about how children learn with computers.

Not only were teachers excluded from the perspectives of technology researchers during this period, but schools were usually excluded as well. However, during the late 1980s and early 1990s, school reformers who were also interested in technology began to recognize that the structure and culture of schools limited possibilities for creating environments where students could learn higher order thinking skills. Those unwilling to dispose so easily of the teacher's role envisioned that computers would foster teachers' ability to design individualized, independent learning environments. Many predicted that computers would upset traditional classroom routines, but continued to conceive the teacher's role as central.

Practitioners and researchers began to think about the potential influences of computer technology on classroom and school culture and about how this might intersect with calls for school reform and restructuring. Computers might catalyze restructuring by symbolizing change, inviting new ways of thinking, forcing increased collaboration between teachers in order to learn the technology, and engendering new roles and relationships in the classroom (Collins, 1990; David, 1990; Dede, 1990; Sheingold, 1990). An important critique of this thinking held that computers would likely serve merely to amplify existing practice; in and of themselves they would not change teaching in any way (Cohen, 1987; Cuban, 1986).

Though it is clear that most teachers will continue to struggle with how to integrate computers into their teaching, the knowledge base for this integration is growing. Through the hard work of researchers who utilize cognitive science to develop new software, educators who develop new computer-based curricula, scholars who conduct research on the integration of technology into schools, and the many teachers who work with computers daily in classrooms, this knowledge is increasing over time. Still, many problems remain, and communities continue to increase their demand that teachers make use of computers in teaching.

With all the challenges and costs involved, the question of *how* the computers are used—the quality of their use—becomes paramount. Few studies have successfully linked increased student achievement to computer use. (For an exception, see Wenglinsky, 1998.) One reason for this may be that alternative assessments are more appropriate than standardized tests for measuring the learning resulting from students' use of computers, and thus standard measures fail to reflect actual improvements (Honey, Culp, & Spielvogel, 1999).

## Linking Computers to Constructivist Teaching

Given these tentative assessment results, one way to promote quality is to link computers to a promising practice. A broad consensus has emerged among educators that a kind of teaching, called *constructivism*, or "teaching for understanding," is required to develop lasting knowledge, understanding, and higher level thinking (see, for example, Anderson, 1985; Bransford, Brown, & Cocking, 1999; Brown & Duguid, 1989; Cohen, McLaughlin, & Talbert, 1993; Gardner, 1985; Resnick, 1987; Wiske, 1998). This approach is based on findings in cognitive psychology since the late 1960s. Distinct from traditional pedagogy and instructional design, constructivist teaching is characterized by classroom activities that foster students' active engagement with material and mimic real-world situations to promote thinking skills and emphasize conceptual over rote learning.

In traditional pedagogy, knowledge is conceived as discrete facts commonly understood by everyone, and knowledge is fixed, something we can all point to and understand in the same way. For *constructivists*, on the other hand, learners build on experience and existing knowledge, such that symbols are of a more personal nature, understood slightly differently by each individual. An important part of learning, then, becomes the coconstruction of disciplinary meaning (Duffy & Jonassen, 1992; Gardner, 1991; Jonassen, 1996; Scardamalia, Bereiter, McLean, et al., 1991–92). For constructivists, learning is an active process during which the student continually develops and refines interpretive frameworks for knowledge (Borko & Putnam, 1996; Bruner, 1966). The learner does not separate knowledge from the context in which it is learned; rather, knowledge is intimately connected to specific settings and embedded within particular applications (Brown & Duguid, 1989). "Teachers using a constructivist approach realize that learning is not only a matter of transferring ideas from one who is knowledgeable to one who is not," write Sandholtz, Ringstaff, and Dwyer. "Instead, learning is perceived as a personal, reflective, and transformative process where ideas, experiences, and points of view are integrated and something new is created— a view where teacher work is construed as facilitating individuals' abilities to construct knowledge" (1997, p. 12).

Classroom activities guided by the constructivist paradigm differ from the traditional didactic model, as do teachers' and students' roles. In constructivist classrooms, teachers design activities to relate abstract concepts to phenomena in the real world and to students' prior experience. In order to accomplish this, teachers become more facilitators and coaches, less dispensers of knowledge, and learning becomes more individualized. Constructivism emphasizes teaching that provides mental scaffolding for students, generating activities that will guide them in building their own knowledge and understanding. Students, according to this model, must actively work on their own learning and help one another. In practice, this means that teachers usually employ a combination of techniques. Sometimes they present concepts and information to students, but the backbone of their teaching consists of long-term assignments embedding opportunities to learn important concepts and strengthen understanding.

Historically, the higher order thinking skills promoted by this paradigm have always been accessible to a small segment of the population. But the call for teaching higher order skills to students on a mass basis poses a new challenge for educators. What is new in the present era, according to Lauren Resnick (1987), is that more educators are now committed to making thinking and problem solving a regular part of a school program for all of the population, including children of color, those who learn English as a second language, and students of low socioeconomic background. "It is a new challenge to develop educational programs that assume that all individuals, not just an elite, can become competent thinkers" (pp. 6–7).

This view has become more developed and more popular as it has been adopted by national networks such as the National Council of Teachers of

Mathematics, by major standards, curriculum, and assessment projects such as New Standards, by many university-sponsored projects throughout the country such as Project Zero, as well as by an increasing number of teacher preparation programs. Most recently, the National Academy of Sciences demonstrated a clear interest in the approach by publishing a book on the relationship between cognitive science, curriculum, and schooling (Bransford et al., 1999).

## Technology and School Reform

As efforts to use computers in classrooms proceeded, educational practitioners, researchers, and policymakers became aware that using technology to support high-quality, high-level teaching and learning is inextricably intertwined with school reform as a whole (Collins, 1990; Glennan & Melmed, 1996; Means & Olson, 1995; Sheingold, 1990). A report by Glennan and Melmed, published by RAND in 1996, proposes a national strategy for technology and recommends introducing educational technology into schools "as a component of a broader effort of school reform," which, its authors argue, would include developing high standards, creating assessments to effectively measure those standards, changing the role of teachers, providing students more time for learning, and adopting engaging instructional practices (p. xix). They write that "in the absence of changes in the incentives governing the behavior of schools and teachers, it is unlikely that student learning will improve. Technology without reform is likely to have little value; widespread reform without technology is probably impossible" (pp. xix–xx).

Research on how schools can support the use of computer technology for instruction have linked effective use to several main organizational conditions: a critical ratio of computers to students that approximates 1:4, time and support for teachers to learn to use the technology, technical support readily available within the school, and scheduling and time flexibility (David, 1990; Glennan & Melmed, 1996; Means & Olson, 1995; U.S. Congress, 1995). But even though these factors may be necessary prerequisites for schoolwide technology use and integration, they have no necessary relationship to the details of how teachers will employ the technology, whether they will do so well, or how they will master the complex process of integration.

Means and Olson (1995) conducted case studies of nine schools that were using technology for what they call "technology-supported constructivist classrooms." The teachers in their study felt that technology use strengthened students' sense of authenticity about their work, raised the level of complexity students could handle, and instigated increased collaboration between students. The teachers involved felt that their work on integration helped them to adopt more of a coaching and advisory role in the classroom.

Among the characteristics that facilitated successful implementation of technology in these schools were: development of a shared schoolwide vision, time for teachers to learn to use the technology and incorporate it into their practice, rewards and recognition for exemplary activities, a structure within which teachers can innovate, partnering with outside resources for money or knowledge, and opportunities for teacher collaboration. Although Means and Olson successfully examine the links between technology use and constructivist-based teaching, they do not specifically address the issue of *how* teachers learned to change their teaching practice in these schools.

Several studies have examined specifically how teachers use technology to support constructivist teaching (Becker, 1994; Glennan & Melmed, 1996; Means & Olson, 1995; Sandholtz et al., 1997), and have examined how an individual teacher in a classroom learns to do so. However, we now need to know more about the relationship between teachers' learning processes and the school organization.

## Restructuring for Teacher Learning and Professional Growth

Constructivist teaching using computers often requires that teachers teach in ways that few have learned either in professional preparation programs or during their own experience as students in K–12 classrooms. And school-based professional development still occurs most commonly in the form of workshops, which assume teachers will absorb the ideas presented and then enact them in their classrooms. Increasingly, research on professional development suggests that teachers should learn new practices right in the workplace, yet traditional schools provide few opportunities for such learning. While much traditional professional development for teachers takes the form of one-shot sessions, in-service days, or unspecified coursework, researchers and practitioners increasingly view professional development that is episodic or removed in any way from daily classroom practice as ineffective, favoring instead developmental experiences grounded in the teachers' daily classroom work (Darling-Hammond & McLaughlin, 1996; Lieberman, 1996).

Often isolated from one another by the architecture of schools, where they spend most of their day as the only adult among many children, teachers have few chances to observe their colleagues teaching, see new instructional approaches, or receive feedback from colleagues (Goodlad, 1984; Lortie, 1975; Rosenholtz, 1991; Sarason, 1990; Sizer, 1985). Moreover, few teachers can spend solitary time during the workday to reflect quietly on teaching, to study content or new instructional practices, or simply to polish a lesson (Hargreaves, 1993).

If teacher learning is to take place within the context of the school and not outside it in separate professional development sessions, the design and culture of the school organization must support this learning. Several writers argue that only when schools become "learning organizations" (Senge, 1990) or "learning communities," where adults learn as well as students, will we see genuine, productive change in classroom practice (Fullan, 1993, 1995; Sarason, 1990). Though this notion is extremely popular, especially among education reformers, clear conceptions of what this might mean are just being developed.

What would such schools look like? From the late 1980s until the present, educators have tinkered with the structure of schools, hoping that increased preparatory time for teachers, opportunities to work collaboratively, smaller class sizes, smaller personalized groups for students, and longer class periods would yield desired improvements in school climate and academic achievement (Tyack & Cuban, 1997). Several recent studies have examined this type of restructuring in order to evaluate whether these approaches actually improve schools. In a meta-analysis of data on school organization and restructuring, Newmann and Wehlage (1995) emphasize that if there is a "solution" to the problem of successfully restructuring schools, it lies with placing student learning at the center of the picture, surrounding it with agreement among adults about what constitutes authentic pedagogy, creating organizational elements that support professional community among teachers, and maintaining an external policy environment that is supportive of school efforts.

In a study of three restructuring schools, Elmore, Peterson, & McCarthey (1996) found that restructuring in and of itself did not lead to improvement in instruction. Rather, they saw instructional improvement in the schools where teachers shared a common vision of good teaching and there was sustained attention to improving instructional practice. For the best results, they write, "Teachers need direct experience with the kind of practice they are expected to engage in, either by working with an expert or by being in an organization in which the practice is part of the air they breathe" (p. 233). They conclude that changes in school structure do not necessarily lead to improvement in teaching practice and recommend that "providing access to new knowledge and skill for teachers should supersede attention to the problem of how to restructure schools" (p. 242).

To look at how people interact and learn from one another requires moving from analyses of organizational structure to examining a school's professional culture. What elements of a school's cultural environment support teachers' professional learning? Sarason (1990) argues that to create schools where children can learn, adults must exist in a "technical culture" that is both intellectually challenging and personally satisfying. These conditions for adults in schools, he asserts, are prerequisites to creating the same successful learning conditions for students. Along the same lines, Fullan (1993,

1995) promotes a vision of school organizations as places where continuous learning is a strongly supported norm for both students and staff.

This empirical and theoretical literature points to the centrality of teacher learning for improving instructional practice. It also raises questions about what aspects of school organizations might promote teacher learning and improvement.

## NEW APPROACHES: MERGING SCHOOL REFORM, STANDARDS, AND TECHNOLOGY

Recently, research perspectives have come to merge several aspects of computer use in schools, evolving into a more holistic, instructionally oriented stance. In 1997, Sandholtz, Ringstaff, and Dwyer published *Teaching with Technology*, which describes how teachers in the Apple Classrooms of Tomorrow (ACOT) learned to incorporate computers and other technologies into their teaching when immersed in a technology-intensive environment. Researchers on the project found that the availability of technology alongside appropriate organizational support had a significant impact on how teaching and learning occurred in the computer-rich classrooms. They watched expert teachers work with technology in classrooms, plan for technology use in their own curriculum, and receive ongoing support as they transferred what they had learned to their own practice. The ACOT studies have provided an interesting model of professional development involving visitation, modeling, and situated coaching of teachers learning to use technology. Although the authors of this study made recommendations regarding support for technology use, they did not specifically study schoolwide integration of technology and so were unable to comment on the overall contextual and cultural environment that would support it.

In *The Connected School: Technology and Learning in High School* (2001), Means, Penuel, and Padilla studied six urban, computer-using high schools to discover what barriers and supports for technology integration existed in these schools. Many of these barriers to "student-empowering uses" of technology were in fact resolved by the public school that I describe in this book. Means and her colleagues argue that "a pedagogical vision for technology use" is essential. In this volume I explore what leadership at one school has done to make sure that such a vision exists.

*The Digital Classroom: How Technology Is Changing the Way We Teach and Learn* (Gordon, 2000), is an excellent edited compilation of articles addressing the intersection of teaching, learning, school management, and technology use. This book hits key issues in the field of technology integration, particularly in pointing out that technology use is inextricable from pedagogical concerns. It is an example of how thinking in the field has evolved to examine how pedagogy and technology use are intertwined.

John LeBaron and Catherine Collier have edited a book featuring short articles on a range of schools that participate in the International Network of Principal's Centers. *Technology in Its Place: Successful Technology Infusion in Schools* (2001) describes settings where practitioners are beginning to understand the connection between pedagogy and technology, discussing curriculum integration and leadership strategies for promoting it.

Most important perhaps, this book takes up a challenge posed by Larry Cuban in *Teachers and Machines: The Classroom Use of Technology Since 1920* (Cuban, 1986) and, more recently, in *Oversold and Underused: Computers in the Classroom* (2001). This book addresses Cuban's important challenge to the widespread assumption that the presence of computer technology will alter instruction. In *Oversold and Underused,* Cuban argues that technology is likely not worth the large investment of funds required, because the machines are not well-used in the schools he studied, seldom linked to any deep changes in the schools or in teaching, and draw resources from other, more valuable reforms such as lowering class size.

This study approaches the issue from a different angle: The needs and developing theories and practices of instruction are what will actually drive improvement and change in classrooms, but computers are a new and vital resource in this change. They provide what Jonassen (1996) calls "mindtools," assisting cognition by supporting our thinking. Computers do not change teaching or schools; they are, after all, inanimate objects. But they can be powerful tools when teachers see them as a possible solution to an identified pedagogical issue. Here, I address Cuban's challenge by accepting that having computers in the classroom does not initiate changes in teaching. Rather, I look closely at the intersection between pedagogy and computers, and what elements in the school organization are most promising for the use of computers to improve teaching.

# CHAPTER 2

# Keeping Your Eye on the Ball: Instruction at the Center of School Organization

CONSTRUCTIVIST TEACHING with computers is a powerful pedagogy that many educators and citizens aspire to see in their schools. But to attain it, they will have to focus on it, and require the school organization to fully enable that focus. Therefore, the challenge for educational leaders is how to keep instructional practice *the* central concern as they design policy systems, lead organizations, and play out the complexities of life in schools. This has prompted Martha Stone Wiske to advise school leaders to "keep your eye on the ball" when advocating the use of classroom technology.

How can educators create schools and systems that consistently support high-quality, powerful learning? What does it mean to create an environment that fosters pedagogical excellence and continuous learning for faculty? Here, I have tackled these questions as a topic of research by focusing on how one particular school has developed its practice of constructivist teaching with computers. These findings should illuminate how pedagogy, teacher learning, and organization relate to one another. The challenge for educational leaders is how to keep instructional practice *the* central concern as they design policy systems, lead organizations, and play out the complexities of life in schools. And therefore, the challenge for researchers is to create analytical models grounded in the real experience of schools that extend the leaders' understanding of school organization and what it means to place instruction central.

An analysis of how organizational culture influences teaching with computers also requires placing instruction squarely at the center of the analysis. This is no longer an unusual approach; scholars and practitioners of administration and policy increasingly situate instructional practice in classrooms at the center of their work. Previous emphases on such matters as school climate, control, and discipline have not yielded desired outcomes in the form of stronger learning for students. *Instructional leadership*—meaning leadership that focuses on the quality of classroom instruction—is thought to be the way to create this focus.

The concept of *backward mapping* in policy studies was originated by Richard Elmore and Milbrey McLaughlin (1988) to emphasize that policies ought to be constructed based on the needs of classroom practice, not the other way around. In a related work, McLaughlin further conceptualized the *embedded contexts* of teaching, arguing that teachers' work is situated within organizational, policy, and community contexts that exert powerful, though mediated, influences on what occurs in the classroom (McLaughlin, Talbert, & Bascia, 1990). Researchers who hope to contribute to improvements in instruction must therefore design studies that begin with an investigation of pedagogical practice before investigating its antecedents.

In order to use a new pedagogical technique, teachers must first learn it themselves. And in order to learn it, these teachers must exist in an organizational environment that is conducive to their learning. Represented graphically, the process would look roughly like the illustration on page 28. The concentric circles signify the embedded contexts in which the practice of instruction exists. At the center is the type of pedagogy that is the central object: a constructivist approach using computers. The next ring describes a condition that is logically necessary for such pedagogy: teacher learning. The outer ring represents the structure and culture of the school organization, which will either support or hinder teachers' ability to learn the new pedagogy. This model keeps instruction at the center of attention, but proposes that organizational culture influences teachers' learning, and that teachers' learning in turn affects classroom practice.

The embedded contexts model serves as the main conceptual model for this study. The design of the research reflected this framework by originating with data collection in classrooms, moving to a study of teachers' learning, then finally to an investigation of the organizational structure and culture that supports such learning and teaching.

"How do teachers learn to use computers for constructivist teaching?" is the first question I explored. Most established teachers have little background in constructivism, relatively little with computers, and almost no experience with a curriculum that fully integrates computers. So, before addressing the larger organizational and policy problem, I needed to understand how teachers learn; their learning is the critical intermediary factor in the process, a precursor to the kind of instruction we want to see.

"Since teacher learning is critical for teaching with computers, what elements of organizational structure and culture promote it?" is the second question posed in this study. I define *organization* to include the structures and culture of the school, the policy environment, and the norms of the

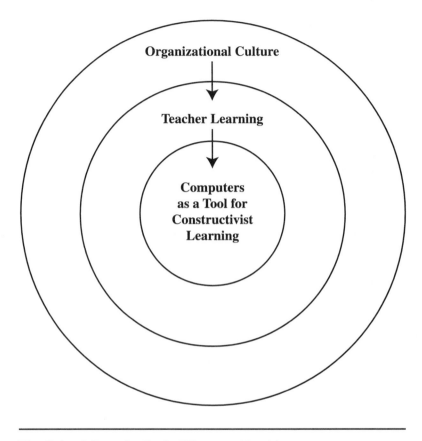

The School Organization's Effects on Teaching

community. Together these establish the resources, incentives, norms, general language, and ways of thinking within a school. Together they shape
much of what occurs, what is possible—and impossible.

## RESEARCHING INSTRUCTION IN CONTEXT: MOVING FROM THE CENTER OUTWARD

The design of this study reflects the necessity to examine school organization from the perspective of its core function, instructional practice (Elmore
& Burney, 1997). I began with a focus on the work of five teachers who were

chosen because they were using computers for constructivist-style pedagogy in different subjects and in different ways. I observed their work in the classroom so as to understand what they were doing and how it affected their students. I then asked how they understood the work they did; most specifically, I sought their stories about how they learned to do it. In response to the very simple question, "How did you learn to do this?" they each related a particular, individual story. In the end, through analyzing these stories as five case studies, I found common predispositions and processes among them, but no common techniques or prescriptions.

What they did have in common was that they worked in the same school and therefore labored each day within the same organizational culture, even though that culture itself was complex and varied, not a uniform entity. Logically, the next step was to move to the peripheral circle in my model, to gather data about how the school organization—its structure and culture—promoted, impeded, or otherwise affected their learning. I did this by asking them about their experience at the school (What's it like to work here? What's valued here?) and their understanding of its subtleties (How do you get ahead here?). I explored their every mention of professional learning by attempting to connect their experience to the organizational environment. (How did you get to go to that conference? Did you get a day off? Who paid for it? What happened when you came back? Did you talk to anyone about it? In what way? Did you use anything in the classroom? What happened next?) In this way I came to understand their versions of professional learning. At the same time, I spoke with a range of teachers other than these five, as well as with administrators, support staff, and community members. I attended events, chatted with students, perused documents, sat in on meetings, conversed in hallways. My own inquiries—what I needed to understand the culture—served as essential data in combination with the perspectives of the teachers to round out a view of this school's ability to promote classroom technology integration.

Educational research that takes an ethnographic approach requires mastering a tension between what we researchers think we know about a subject and opening ourselves to the voices of its participants. It requires knowing what has been studied in the field and what conclusions researchers have reached, then using that knowledge as a kind of mental furniture during ethnographic inquiry. During the inquiry, one can sit a fact or statement down on a chair or sofa to see if it fits comfortably, trying to match the data to notions already established. Sometimes the fit is comfortable; sometimes the chair needs to be moved a bit, perhaps reupholstered; and sometimes the room has to be cleared and redesigned from scratch. But even when a thorough refurbishing is necessary, it is important to know the history of the room and its decor, so improvements can be based on what has come before.

In this spirit, I will discuss next some key findings in the subfields of teacher learning (the inner ring), along with some ideas about the more general field of organizational culture (the outer ring). These ideas and findings will provide a common field of knowledge for the reader, as they did for me when I ventured into the study of teachers' learning and how the organizational environment affects it.

## The Inner Ring: Teacher Learning

A wide range of research depicts a variety of ways in which practicing teachers are thought to learn new instructional practices. The first challenge has been to define *what* teachers learn or need to learn; the next to discover *how* they learn as individuals. The third is to consider what kinds of collegiality and work environments foster their learning.

***Theories, Knowledge, Skills.*** The beliefs teachers hold about their work guide their many decisions, most of which occur moment to moment in the classroom. Calderhead refers to these as "suppositions, commitments, and ideologies" (Calderhead, 1996), indicating that these beliefs consist of theories and ideas about the way teaching and learning work. That there is a connection between teachers' beliefs about learning and their pedagogical decisions was argued by Olson and Bruner in 1996:

> Our interactions with others are deeply affected by our everyday intuitive theories about how our own minds and minds of others work. These theories, rarely made explicit, are omnipresent in practical and educational decisions. . . . Teaching, then, is inevitably based on teachers' notions about the nature of the learner's mind. Beliefs and assumptions about teaching, whether in a school or in any other context, are a direct reflection of the beliefs and assumptions the teacher holds about the learner. (pp. 10–11)

Some of these theories are explicit and others tacit. Explicit theories are the ones a teacher can state outright, while tacit theories may only be detected through watching a teacher's activities or when teachers are questioned about particular decisions made in the classroom. Two researchers who study teachers' professional learning argue that an important component of pedagogical knowledge is the "personal theory" of the teacher (Pope & Denicolo, 1986). The theories teachers hold about learning guide their decisions, not only day by day, but also with regard to larger scale decisions about which innovations are worth adopting and which ones should be left aside.

I define *pedagogical theories* as theories that express how a teacher believes children learn and how he or she believes teachers should teach. These theories, whether explicit or tacit, constitute the mental landscape a teacher uses to make countless decisions over the course of a class period, a day, a semester, a year, and a career. They guide decisions about everything over which the teacher has control: setting up a classroom's physical space, rules of conduct, curriculum, texts and resources, assignments, groupings, how to ask a question, how to answer a question, what grades to give, how to respond to homework, how hard to push a student, how structured to be, or how loose. The teachers in this study related every decision they made in the classroom to the question, "How will this affect my students' learning?" How they define the scope of this question and how they answer it constitutes their pedagogical philosophy.

Without arguing that any individual buys a set of beliefs wholesale, it does seem that constructivist teachers subscribe to a group of beliefs about the nature of knowledge, the process of learning, and the practice of teaching that contrasts with the beliefs of more traditional teachers, who are often termed *objectivist*, on these topics. Constructivist teachers believe, for example, that learning is an active process during which the student develops and refines interpretive frameworks into which he or she can store factual or other knowledge (Borko & Putnam, 1996; Bruner, 1966). This is a highly active, individual process, which implies that each person makes meaning of the knowledge presented in his or her own way to conduct a highly personalized cognitive framework. Traditional teachers, on the other hand, tend to believe that knowledge is an external entity, something one can point to, and that the role of the teacher is to convey this knowledge to children. The idea within this system of beliefs is that everyone "knows" the same things. Some may know already, and some may not know yet, but the same knowledge is out there to be gained.

Since objectivist teachers believe that knowledge is a definable entity that can be conveyed to children, they generally hold the concept that curriculum, pace, and direction of instruction should follow a predetermined path. Constructivist teachers, by contrast, believe that students' ideas should to some extent guide what goes on in the classroom (Lampert, 1993; Nelson & Hammerman, 1996; Sandholtz et al., 1997; Wiske & Houde, 1993). Constructivist teachers confer more intellectual authority to students, whereas traditional teachers retain that authority (M. S. Wiske, personal communication, December 1996). Constructivists embed material within larger thematic units or projects (Lampert, 1993; Spillane & Jennings, 1995; Wiske & Houde, 1993; Wiske, Niguidula, & Shepard, 1988), while traditional teachers tend to present material in discrete units.

Constructivist teaching requires that the teacher possess extensive and deep knowledge of both subject matter and pedagogy. This knowledge is especially necessary in constructivist classrooms where discourse is opened up to the questioning and inquiry of the students. Teachers need content knowledge sufficient to field questions, address misconceptions, guide the discourse in productive directions, and connect students' ideas to the curricular agenda (Darling-Hammond, 1995; Shulman, 1986, 1987; Wiske, 1998). As they work with students, they must model an understanding of the rules for valid disciplinary knowledge. And they need pedagogical knowledge about the most effective ways to teach key concepts in a discipline—how to represent, exemplify, and help students tie concepts together.

In addition to these beliefs and knowledge, teaching for understanding with technology, in particular, requires teachers to master challenging management and pedagogical skills. Classroom management strategies must shift when lectures become less prominent and are replaced by students working independently or in small groups (Lampert, 1993; Sandholtz et al., 1997; Wiske & Houde, 1993; Wiske et al., 1988).

When teachers use computers in the classroom, they must know how to manage computer hardware and how to work with students who are learning software. In addition, teachers must develop considerable skill in matching the capability of computer software to instructional needs (Perkins, Schwartz, West, & Wiske, 1995; Schwartz, 1995). They must learn how to employ the technology in ways that promote learning, for example, by choosing specific exercises within curricular software, knowing how to pattern students' writing process to take advantage of word processing capabilities, wrapping a lesson around a computer simulation, or structuring students' use of the Internet for research. This type of teaching generally requires complex forms of assessment designed to demonstrate understanding and the ability to reason within a subject (Honey et al., 1999).

Constructivist, computer-using teachers find themselves overseeing multiple strands of activity and many different tasks. They must cultivate independent work habits in their students, as well as the confidence to generate new ideas. Working with computers in classrooms often introduces new complexity to the task of teaching (Lampert, 1993; Sandholtz et al., 1997; Wiske & Houde, 1993; Wiske et al., 1988).

**Study, Reflection, Inquiry.** Prior research points to three main avenues by which experienced teachers learn: individual study of content and pedagogical knowledge, reflection on teaching practice, and inquiry into aspects of teaching that emerge as problematic.

Knowledge of content and pedagogy may be obtained through individual study, which includes reading, discussion of readings, and taking courses. It may also include observing other teachers or obtaining exposure to alternative instructional approaches through colleagues or networks (Darling-Hammond, 1995; Lieberman, 1996; McLaughlin & Oberman, 1996).

Another important way teachers learn is by reflecting on problematic incidents or searching for resolution to puzzles in their teaching (Cinnamond & Zimpher, 1990; Grimmett & Erickson, 1988; Grimmett, MacKinnon, Erickson, & Riecken, 1990; Schön, 1983, 1987, 1988). Donald Schön (1983), who is credited with developing this concept, defines *reflection* as how professionals think about events that have occurred in the course of their practice and how and what they have meant for desired results. Grimmett and associates (1990) divide the idea of reflection into three types, based on studies of teachers' reflective practice: (1) putting educational research or theory into practice; (2) deliberating among competing views of teaching; and (3) reorganizing or reconstructing experience in ways that lead to new understandings of situations. Cinnamond and Zimpher point out that reflectivity, where it occurs, comes from living in a community of practitioners: "Reflection does not occupy a separate place in social processes, but is already embedded in them."

Inquiring into aspects of one's own or another's teaching means puzzling through an aspect of practice that yields unexpected or unsatisfactory results. It differs from reflection because *inquiry* implies systematic research into a subject. In the inquiry process, teachers pursue resources such as information or expertise to help them develop solutions to a particular teaching challenge. This may be done through looking to external or internal resources.

Study, reflection, and inquiry may each be pursued alone or with other people. They may also be combined. For example, if a novice teacher observes an experienced one, and they together reflect on the class that was observed, it would be a form of study for the novice, and reflection for the mentor.

### The Outer Ring: Organizational Culture

What organizational conditions, then, provide a conducive environment for teachers to continuously improve their teaching practice within a system of beliefs that makes knowledge personal, requires tremendous content mastery and flexibility by the teacher, and, in addition, seeks to integrate new technologies that are powerful but often mysterious and difficult? That the conditions in the average school are not conducive to such learning is accepted by virtually every school reformer, whether researcher or practitioner.

Scholars have written extensively regarding the importance of collegial environments for teacher learning. Research provides evidence connecting a high level of collegiality and professional community to teachers' perceptions that they are learning, and even to improved student achievement (Newmann & Wehlage, 1995; Rosenholtz, 1991). Such collegial learning might occur during interactions at school, either within formal structures established by the school such as professional development sessions, or via informal patterns of communication loosely based on departmental organization, classroom proximity, friendships, interdisciplinary teaching groups, or teacher networks outside of the school (Darling-Hammond & McLaughlin, 1996; Lieberman, 1988, 1996; Little, 1982, 1993; Siskin, 1994).

In 1991, Susan Rosenholtz published a very thorough study that related organizational conditions to teacher learning. She explicitly examined teachers' "opportunities for learning" in elementary schools and found that they were highest in places where teachers were involved with setting school goals related to instruction, when supervision and evaluation systems aligned with and supported those goals, and where teachers collaborated frequently around issues of practice. Rosenholtz argues that in schools where learning opportunities for teachers are frequent, and collegiality between the teachers is high, "there are organizational signals beckoning for greater professional growth to better meet the challenge of students whose learning requirements still exceed teachers' collective grasp" (p. 99). Using a survey measure of how much opportunity teachers had to learn, Rosenholtz found that 79% of the variation in learning opportunities among teachers were explained by four organizational characteristics:

1. Goal-setting activities that emphasize specific instructional objectives
2. Focused, high-quality, and frequent supervision and evaluation by principals, who identify instructional issues and monitor teachers' progress
3. Shared teaching goals among faculty, which "create pressure to conform to norms of school renewal"
4. "Collaboration that at once enables and compels teachers to offer and request advice in helping each other improve instructionally" (pp. 102–103)

In Rosenholtz's study, the opportunity to share with colleagues was most important in schools that encouraged experimentation and provided support and encouragement for risk taking. In these schools, practice was not viewed as private, and school norms allowed for teachers to request help from others and offer help to others. In schools that were low on Rosenholtz's scales of learning or collegiality, norms of collegial interaction tended to value self-reliance; asking for or offering help was considered a violation of this norm. The higher learning schools had altered that norm because teachers in these schools held common goals, which mitigated the occurrence of separate, independent agendas. When goal setting, socialization, and evaluation were not aligned, "faculties fracture[d] into atoms with entirely separate orbits, a mélange of teaching definitions, goals, and indicators of success" (p. 18).

In schools with low levels of collegial interaction, Rosenholtz found that teachers said they had no time before, during, or after school for interaction with colleagues. Yet, almost all the teachers in collaborative settings reported that interactions with colleagues were extremely important to them. The teachers in the collaborative settings more often reported a departure time of 5:00 P.M., while teachers in noncollaborative settings often reported leaving school at 3:00 P.M.

Newmann and Wehlage, in their 1995 study on restructuring schools, similarly found that goal alignment and the presence of professional community were associated with student achievement. In the schools that worked well, they found that goals, supervision, and work activities were more tightly joined than in average schools. These findings, in turn, reinforce Schein's (1992) argument that in order to get members of an organization to undertake difficult learning, the organization must simultaneously capture their attention through incentive structures, while providing a safe and productive environment for learning.

Brown and Duguid (1991) emphasize that successful workplace learning is contextual and attempts to separate learners from the context of their practice (as workshops and training seminars do) should be viewed with caution. The communities of practice that are relevant to learning "are often noncanonical and not recognized by the organization. They are more fluid and interpenetrative than bounded, often crossing the restrictive boundaries of the organization to incorporate people from outside" (p. 49). Brown and Duguid encourage researchers to examine work practice and learning "not in terms of the groups that are ordained (e.g., 'task forces' or 'trainees') but in terms of the communities that emerge" (p. 49).

Subgroups exist within any school, although they can be expected to vary in their culture and in the degree of collegial interaction they provide (Little, 1981; Siskin & Little, 1995; Talbert, 1995). In some cases, precisely which reference groups are important for a particular teacher in his or her daily work may be discovered by analyzing the formal organizational structure. In high schools, for example, the subject department is usually a very important reference group having distinct culture and norms. In other cases, however, the most important reference group may be one that was informally created—perhaps through friendships—or ad hoc in nature, such as a group working jointly on a particular project. The variability in these communication and collegial patterns requires that, as part of any research on schools, they be uncovered for the particular place and for the particular teachers involved.

In addition to research specifically on school organizations, a review of more general organizational theory is helpful here as well. Like other organizations, a school is defined by its structure and culture. The structure defines what's possible physically, through allocation of resources and constructions of power. Structures form the backbone of an organization. They consist of hard organizational qualities like hierarchies, power arrangements, resources, and incentive structures (Bolman & Deal, 1991; Mintzberg, 1979). For schools in particular, the structure consists of daily realities such as the physical plant, equipment, resources for books and instructional materials, staffing, salaries, organization of work, organization of time, and grouping of students (Elmore, 1995).

Culture is the softer part of the organization; it is in the realm of ideas and norms. It defines what is possible through combining the construction of normative ideas with social feedback for what people say and do. What is the usual way of thinking about something, and how is it framed? What is considered normal behavior within the group and what is considered deviant? What kinds of things can be said and done that remain within the frame of what is acceptable? What behavior allows one to remain in the group, and what gets one ejected? Norms define the boundaries—the range of acceptable behavior. Values define what is admired in the group, what solidifies one's membership and raises one's status. Mental theories are another important aspect of culture, especially so when we talk about schools as workplaces devoted to learning. Theories are mental frameworks that define how people understand their work. When they are shared, they come to constitute a shorthand and include a language that signifies shared conceptions. (See Cole & Scribner, 1974; D'Andrade, 1995; Swidler, 2001.)

Edgar Schein's definition of organizational culture emphasizes how it functions to create coherence:

> The most useful way to think about culture is to view it as the accumulated shared learning of a given group, covering behavioral, emotional, and cognitive elements of the group members' total psychological functioning. . . . [T]here must be a history of shared experience, which in turn implies some stability of membership in the group. Given such stability and a shared history, the human need for parsimony, consistency, and meaning will cause the various shared elements to form into patterns that eventually can be called a culture. (1992, p. 10)

Although beginning with this general description, Schein also acknowledges the theoretical controversy regarding whether a group has a single coherent culture by noting that not all groups develop coherent cultures, and that within many organizations subcultures too may develop. Even a relatively coherent culture is quite difficult to characterize. Still, drawing from a wide range of sources, Schein outlines ten dimensions that are valuable for understanding the ways in which organizational culture is expressed:

- *Observed behavioral regularities*: forms of interaction, language, rituals;
- *Espoused values*: the articulated, publicly announced principles and values that the group claims to be trying to achieve;
- *Formal philosophy*: the policies and ideological principles that guide a group's actions toward stakeholders;
- *Climate*: the feeling that is conveyed in a group by the physical layout and the way in which members of the organization interact with each other . . . or with . . . outsiders;
- *Embedded skills*: the special competencies group members display in accomplishing certain tasks, the ability to pass certain things from generation to generation without this necessarily being articulated in writing;
- *Rules of the game*: the implicit rules for getting along in the organization, "the ropes" that a newcomer must learn to become an accepted member;
- *Group norms*: implicit standards and values;
- *Habits of thinking, mental models, and/or linguistic paradigms*: the shared cognitive frames that guide the perceptions, thought, and languages used by the members of a group and taught to new members in the early socialization process;
- *Shared meanings*: the emergent understandings that are created by group members as they interact with each other;
- *"Root metaphors" or integrating symbols*: the ideas, feelings, and images groups develop to characterize themselves, that may or may not be appreciated consciously. (pp. 8–9)

Schein argues that organizational culture develops in response to the organization's need to survive. It must find ways to adapt to its external environment, and to integrate internal processes. For the organization's survival, it is critical that it balance the needs of multiple stakeholders. Schein describes the process organizations use to work on these problems as a "cycle," the elements of which may be addressed simultaneously or separately. Organizations must develop a strategy such that members obtain a shared understanding of their core mission, primary tasks, and obvious and more latent functions. Members must also develop a consensus on goals as they are derived from the core mission.

Culture provides a powerful, pervasive context that shapes the work of an organization through a combination of framing and sanctions. However, individuals—with their unique histories, perspectives, and personalities— operate within this general framework so that the culture should not be thought of as deterministic, but rather as highly influential. In a school, the culture—and structure—is the field of play on which teachers and students work and learn. Its contours define what is considered right, what is considered important, what is considered normal.

Management writers such as Tom Peters, Robert Waterman, and Peter Senge argue that successful organizations build cohesive cultures around common norms, values, and ideas (Peters, 1988; Peters & Waterman, 1988; Senge, 1990). Scholars of education likewise argue that the creation of a culture that supports teaching and learning is a necessary part of school leadership (e.g., Deal & Peterson, 1999; Sergiovanni, 2000). For a school, this consensus would mean agreeing on which students the school is really meant to educate, in what subjects, and to what level. "One of the most central elements of any culture," Schein writes, "will be the assumptions the members of the organization share about their identity and ultimate mission or function" (1992, p. 56).

It is unusual, however, for schools to have a culture that nurtures adult learning. Since this book focuses on a single school, it would be helpful to set it against a backdrop of more typical high schools. Several important studies conducted during the 1980s provide a background description of the typical comprehensive high school. Schools are certainly different in many ways than they were in the 1980s, yet most of their key elements remain astoundingly constant. The way students are organized (grades, subjects, levels), the way teachers work (courses, classrooms, mostly alone, pressed for time), the content of the curriculum, and main forms of assessment (tests) have remained remarkably stable. Research on the character of high school provides a background against which to understand Woodland High School, the subject of this study. Woodland is a typical comprehensive high school in many ways, yet many aspects of its structure and culture differ from the norm. What is important to learn from this study is how those differences (and perhaps similarities) enable the ability of teachers at Woodland to learn a challenging new practice, constructivist teaching with computers.

## BACKGROUND KNOWLEDGE: THE BASELINE SCHOOL

The structure of a school includes how teachers' classes and preparatory time are scheduled, the school's physical design, space available to teachers, teaching loads, and the availability of any personnel (such as professional developer, coach, coteacher, or mentor) who may impact teachers' learning. These aspects are often referred to as "the regularities of schooling" (Elmore, 1995; Sarason, 1996). A school's structure also includes its organization into subject area departments, houses, and committees. Subject departments in the high school, in particular, constitute highly salient professional communities for teachers (Johnson, 1990; Siskin & Little, 1995). Formal groups set up by the school, including departments, teaching teams, houses, or committees, may be one source of learning. In other cases the most important reference group may be informal (such as friendships) or ad hoc (a group working on a project).

The structure of most schools reinforces a sense of isolation in one's work, or what Seymour Sarason (1996) calls "aloneness." Although teachers spend large amounts of time in the presence of students, they spend relatively little conversing with other adults. "Teachers are alone with their children and problems in a classroom," Sarason writes, "and the frequency and pattern of contact with others like themselves are a kind and quality that make new learning and change unlikely" (p. 134). Lortie (1975) argues that the historic schoolhouse model of self-contained classrooms grew into the "egg crate school," in which teachers pursue their work, each in his or her own classroom, working in the same building, but not interacting much. "Throughout the long, formative decades of the modern school system, schools were organized around teacher separation rather than teacher interdependence" (p. 14). He goes on to establish a portrait of the secondary school that still rings true today.

> Secondary schooling . . . would mix notions of serial learning and contemporaneous study of different subjects. This type of organization meant that each teacher was assigned specific areas of responsibility and was expected to teach students the stipulated knowledge and skills without assistance from others. . . . The growth pattern and organization of public schools have accommodated to these conditions. It was easier for those governing schools to see them as aggregates of classroom units, as collections of independent cells, than as tightly integrated "organisms." They could cope with expansion of the student population by adding new classrooms and new teachers—it was not always necessary to create new schools to absorb increased numbers. (pp. 15–16)

The architecture of a school building designed like an egg crate makes informal or serendipitous conversation difficult or unlikely over the course of the school day (Schön, 1988).

Goodlad (1984) describes the intellectual isolation teachers typically experience: "The classroom cells in which teachers spend much of their time appear to be symbolic and predictive of their relative isolation from one another and from sources of ideas beyond their own background of experience" (p. 186). Over 75% of the 1,350 teachers in Goodlad's study of 12 high schools in seven states, in all subjects and teaching all levels, reported that the greatest influences on their teaching was their own background, interests, and experience, as well as students' interests and experiences. They were somewhat influenced by textbooks and curriculum guides, and only minimally influenced by district consultants, outside examinations, or teacher unions. Although they did associate somewhat with other teachers through courses, workshops, and educational organizations, those associations were brief. They rarely worked with other teachers on collaborative endeavors such as committees, projects, exchanges with other schools, or projects within their school. In the schools described by Goodlad, there were few infrastructures designed to encourage or support communication among teachers about their teaching, augmenting their professional and intellectual isolation.

The flip side of this isolation may be the strong sense of autonomy felt by teachers regarding their work. Powell, Farrar, and Cohen (1985) report that most teachers in their high school study, which focused on 15 public schools and 4 private ones, said that they had a lot of control in carrying out their jobs, and that their own preparation, experience, and students' interests most strongly influenced what they would teach. "Independence—rather than moral or educational cohesiveness—is a central part of the high school teacher's identity," because "autonomy is one of the few traditionally 'professional' attributes currently possessed by the high school teaching profession" (p. 36). Full faculty meetings in the schools they studied were uncommon, and department meetings dealt mostly with materials allocation or teaching schedules, not educational substance, leaving teachers to their own approach in the classroom.

The way teachers' time is organized also has a large effect on their ability to learn. Goodlad (1984) found that teachers worked a minimum of 37.5 hours per week, a mid-range of 40 to 45 hours per week, to a high of 50 hours per week. The most inflexible portion of the teachers' workday is teaching actual classes. In addition to this assigned time, teachers prepare lessons, correct papers and tests, report student attendance and other data, report to and confer with parents and students, attend meetings, and sometimes handle hall or cafeteria duty. In Goodlad's sample of high school teachers, 40% reported spending 2 to 3 hours per week preparing for each class taught, and another 33% reported spending 4 to 6 hours to prepare for each class. "Clearly," writes Goodlad, "teachers who seek to plan very carefully, to create alternative kinds of classroom activities, or to assign and read essays regularly cannot do what they expect of themselves in a normal week" (p. 170).

The way dedicated teachers reconcile their ideal vision of how much they should prepare their lessons and how carefully they should review students' work, with the reality of demands on their time has become known as "Horace's Compromise," from the book of that title by Ted Sizer (1985). After describing the busy day of a fictional, composite English teacher he calls Horace, Sizer characterizes how Horace must compromise the time he knows he *should* spend critiquing students' writing, with what he finds possible given his student load of 120, five classes per day teaching three different courses, along with other demands on his time. Horace must continually compromise his standards by assigning and reviewing less writing than he knows his students really need. He knows that, as juniors and seniors in high school, his students should be working on essays of a page or two, but due to his time constraints, he assigns just one or two paragraphs. To drive home his point, Sizer gets down to counting minutes:

> Being a veteran teacher, Horace takes only fifteen to twenty minutes to check over each student's daily homework, to read the week's theme, and to write an analysis of it. . . . Horace is realistic: even in his accommodating suburban school, fifteen minutes is too much to spend. He compromises, averaging five minutes for each student's work by cutting all but the most essential corners. . . .
>
> So, to check homework and to read and criticize one paragraph per week per student with the maximum feasible corner-cutting takes six hundred minutes, or ten hours, assuming no coffee breaks or flagging attention. . . .
>
> Horace cares about his teaching and feels that he should take a half-hour to prepare for each class meeting. . . . However, he is realistic. He will compromise by spending no more than ten minutes' preparation time, on average, per class. . . . Three of his sections are ostensibly of the same course, but because the students are different in each case, he knows that he cannot satisfactorily clone each lesson plan twice and teach to his satisfaction. . . .
>
> And so before Horace assigns his one or two paragraphs per week, he is committed for over thirty-two hours of teaching, administration, class preparation, and extracurricular . . . work. Collecting one short piece of writing per week from students and spending a bare five minutes per week on each student's weekly work adds ten hours, yielding a forty-two-hour work week. Lunch periods, supervisory duties frequently, if irregularly, assigned, coffee breaks, travel to and from school, and time for the courtesies, civilities, and biological necessities of life are all in addition. (pp. 17–19)

These studies illustrate the most salient organizational structures in the average American high school. High schools are places where teachers are constrained by time and space, and where teachers generally experience professional isolation from one another. Historically, these organizations have responded by granting—and the teachers have responded by taking—considerable autonomy once the door to the classroom closes.

Woodland High School was able to combine this traditional autonomy with structures and cultural norms that helped teachers learn how to teach with technology. Part II of the book explores how five teachers at Woodland used computers in their classrooms, and how they learned to do so.

# Learning to Teach with Technology: Five Narratives

EACH OF THESE TEACHER'S stories is a narrative that depicts how an individual learns and works within an educational system and a policy system, within a particular community, and in a particular school. The importance of these stories lies in the details they provide about individual learning and development occurring within a cultural and structural context. Each teacher's story has an arc and a logic that describes how his or her learning and classroom work developed over time. As individuals, they have their own predispositions, styles, talents, and interests. Each took a particular learning pathway. Each has strong theories about how students learn and how these theories should guide instruction.

Clifford Geertz (1973) coined the term *thick description* to describe how an anthropologist should work to understand a cultural setting in rich detail. Case studies provide researchers with opportunities to look deeply at how social life works on the ground (Stake, 1995; Yin, 1994). Woodland High School, and five key teachers within it, provide a close look at teacher learning and organizational context. In Part II, I describe the setting of Woodland High School along with the instructional practice and professional learning of five of its computer-using teachers.

The stories should be understood as a thick description of how individual teachers learn to use computers within an organizational and cultural environment. They learn, and mostly teach, as individuals, yet the context within which they work is composed of structural and cultural forces that affect their motivation, focus, and ability to harness resources that will help them learn.

# CHAPTER 3

# Beginning with the Whole: Contexts and Commonalities

TO BE TRUE to the complex reality of how teachers learn to use computers within a school, it is necessary to shuttle between understanding the context of the whole school and understanding the individual learning of each teacher. Returning to the image of concentric circles depicted earlier, we will zoom out to view the larger picture of school context, before we zoom in on the detailed cases for each teacher's instructional practice and professional learning.

## WOODLAND HIGH SCHOOL

Woodland High School (WHS) is located outside a Vermont town in a beautiful setting surrounded by mountains. It is a pleasant place to spend time, with a simple architecture that takes advantage of sunlight and the beautiful outdoors. The people there maintain a relaxed but businesslike atmosphere: no uniforms, plenty of informality between teachers and students, low-key supervision of the hallways, and yet the students are expected to be about business. During free periods or lunch, students may gather in several common areas in the building, which include an outdoor area available during good weather. The library, another place where many students spend time when not in class, has an excellent collection of books and good access to electronic materials. Interactions between adults and students are both respectful and friendly.

I conducted this research during the 1997–98 school year, when 1,062 students attended WHS. According to the school's most recent annual report, it continues to cope with rapidly increasing enrollment, due partly to population increases in the demographic and partly to the general increase in school-age population known as the "baby boomlet." The ethnic composition of the school is more than 90% white, and the towns it serves record lower than a 5% official poverty rate (U.S. Bureau of the Census, 2000). The most significant source of diversity within the school is economic level and educational attainment of parents. Students attend WHS from four different towns and four corresponding feeder schools. Overall, the area feeding the school is affluent relative to the state and nation, but it is important to understand the diversity within the student body in order to grasp the working context for this school. Each of the towns sending children to WHS had populations between 4,000 and 10,000, an overall poverty rate ranging from 2–5%, and a percentage of college-educated adults ranging from 40–59%, as against 29% for the state of Vermont as a whole. In 1999 the median household income in the poorest of the four towns was $8,000 above the national median, and in the wealthiest town, $24,000 above the national median. The official poverty level for families with children under 18 years old among these towns ranged from 0.4% to 8.1%, compared to 13.6% nationally (U.S. Bureau of the Census, 2000). Students and staff at the school understood that the community's families ranged from working and rural to affluent professional. There are some rivalries and identity associations among the four towns served by the school, so that two of them are perceived as wealthier and more professional, and two as poorer and more rural, more working class. This results in subtle but significant dynamics among the students and among the teachers when they discuss their expectations of various students.

Students at WHS consistently achieve better on standard indicators than the state averages, which are, in turn, generally above national averages. In 2000, for example, the national average SAT score was 1013, Vermont's was 1027, and Woodland's was 1093. Again, using the year 1999–2000 as an example, approximately 13% of WHS students took Advanced Placement (AP) exams; and of those tests, 85% of the scores were 3 or above, which is the standard generally used by college admissions committees. The New Standards Reference Exam has been administered in Vermont since 1997–98. This exam is widely considered quite difficult: Students must meet a criterion-referenced benchmark of standards in order to pass. Woodland's 10th grade students meet or exceed the standards of these exams by a significantly higher percentage than the state average. In 2000, on the portion of the test related to mathematics concepts, 19% more of Woodland's students met or exceeded the standard than the average statewide, and 29% more met or exceeded the standard for writing effectiveness in that same year. In 1998, 50% of graduates went on to 4-year colleges; in 1999, 55% did so, and in 2000, 62% did so (WHS, 2002–03).

This data represents a solid level of school achievement in a community with above-average income and education. Based on the data obtained for this study, no direct links can be made between computer use and student achievement. However, it is worthwhile to note that this school served students from diverse socioeconomic backgrounds and still maintained achievement levels and other indicators that were well above average. Within the school, faculty and administration were concerned about the learning of students from the relatively poorer communities, and considered this a significant challenge for the school. The overall intellectual culture and leadership of the school met the challenge of creating and improving strong learning experiences for students. The use of high-quality technology in classrooms is part of the overall pattern of good instruction, high expectations, and keeping learning central.

Serving approximately 1,000 students, Woodland was well staffed during 1997–98, with 70 teachers, 33.5 instructional aides, 4.5 instructional coordinators, 2 licensed administrators, and 52 other personnel such as secretaries, aides, custodial staff, and technologists. Classes ranged widely in size: Some had as many as 60 students with two teachers; others—mostly AP courses—had only a few students and no formal meeting time.

The school ran on a block schedule, which allowed 90 minutes for each class period. Days were designated A-days or B-days, which meant that most subjects met every other day, on either an A or B day. At WHS, while teachers were busy and pressured because of their many activities, I did find that they had relatively more preparation time than teachers in many schools. School opened at 8:00 A.M. and ended at 2:45 P.M. each day, with a 15-minute "call back" until 3 P.M., during which teachers had to be available for students needing additional assistance or conferencing. Of 33.25 possible student contact hours per week at this school, teachers had classes between 19.25 hours and 20.75, depending on whether the week began with an A-day or a B-day. This meant that an average of 59% of their workday was spent in assigned contact with classes of students, leaving about 40% for preparation, committee work, or assisting individual students. This arrangement left teachers considerably more time to pursue professional and curriculum development than in a more typical high school, which might leave as little as 50 minutes per day preparation time, with 20–30 minutes for lunch.

In addition to classes, students and teachers experienced several forms of grouping that defined their lives at school. One form of student grouping provided students with a specified adult advisor through their high school years, which provided teachers with opportunities to work closely with specific students. In the first year, each student was assigned to a faculty advisor. Every day, students attended a 15-minute advisory session, during which teachers made announcements and sometimes sponsored other activities such as providing snacks, organizing charitable work, or discussing events that happened at school or in the community. This block of time allowed the advisor to provide guidance by checking in with students who might be having a hard time, inquiring about attendance issues, addressing problems a student might be having with a particular course, or guiding students wrestling with college applications. The advisory period helped create a climate of personalization, and reinforced a cultural norm that emphasized the importance of serving individual students.

The climate at Woodland was both relaxed and businesslike. Dress was casual; classroom desks might be organized in a wide variety of ways; interactions between students and teachers were respectful, but often informal. Still, it was clear that students and adults alike felt busy, that much was demanded of them, and that being at school meant going about one's business. Teachers treated each other, students, and outsiders (such as a researcher) in a professional manner. From many interactions with faculty, I came to understand that they juggled complex commitments and were often pressured for time. Yet, I found their attitude professional and serious; they made and kept appointments, and came prepared for them. It was clear that, for teachers, students' needs and the demands of teaching were their first priorities. Teachers would always interrupt a conversation with an adult to respond to a student; they were engaged with students throughout class time, and were consistently unwilling to interrupt their work to talk with other adults if they were busy preparing for class.

## PROFESSIONAL LEARNING: COMMONALITIES

How did the teachers within this school learn to use computers for constructivist teaching? I used extensive interviews and classroom observation to elicit their answers to this question, allowing them to paint a picture for me of the sequence, pace, obstacles, and breakthroughs. I tied my questioning to observations of their work with students. For example, after observing a particular classroom session, I would ask such questions as, How did you learn to do that? Why did you set up the activity in that way? Why did you handle that student's question the way you did? What were you thinking about? What will you do next? What do you think went well during this class? What didn't? Then, during longer interviews, I asked each teacher about how he or she began using computers personally or in the classroom, and how what I observed had evolved. From this, each related a story that illustrated an enormously wide range of learning techniques. Some began with personal use; some dove right into the classroom. They learned through courses, reading manuals, professional associations, universities, colleagues, their students, conferences. There was very little mention of in-school courses or workshops, although they had participated in quite a few. Each teacher had an individual story to tell, which I came to think of as their "learning trajectory." How it happened for each individual depended on personal background and schooling, their pathway into the profession, opportunities along the way, their particular subject area, and their own preferences for various learning settings (formal or informal, individual or collective).

But what they had in common were certain dispositions toward learning, which were supported, shaped, and nurtured by the organization and culture. Each story was unique, yet a cross-case analysis of the five showed they shared some common intellectual processes:

- The commitment to use computers
- A definition of pedagogical problems
- Scanning for new ideas and practices
- Creating new curriculum and practice
- Trying, reflecting, refining

The teachers' sense that computers held many possibilities for their classrooms meant they welcomed opportunities to incorporate computers into their teaching. They were committed to the idea of using computers where it made sense. This was a vital step: It seemed the teachers had to make a decision that computers were part of their toolchest before they would explore *how* to use them. Each of the five teachers had developed a strong commitment to using computers over many years, through a combination of growing expertise, exposure to the possibilities of new technologies, and a sense that the school's technological infrastructure and support system made it possible for them to do so. The personal commitment they made, even when not explicit, provided the openness they would need to explore possible uses and the focus they would need to develop and refine new curriculum using technological tools. Other teachers who were ambivalent about or opposed to using computers did not share this conviction.

Administrators and educational policymakers often assume that if teachers are provided hardware, software, and professional development workshops on using computers, they will automatically integrate them into their teaching. When they don't, they are often labeled "resistant to change" (e.g., Huberman & Miles, 1984; Sarason, 1996). In this research, however, I found that teachers' decisions to use or not use computers for a particular segment of curriculum was far more rational than that label would imply: It was based largely on their determination of the pedagogical value added by the technology. This was true for the computer users, the ambivalents, and the nonusers in the study. The difference between them was that regular computer users and ambivalents thought longer and harder about the possible uses before rejecting them. This finding attributes to teachers a high degree of consciousness; a logic rooted in their pedagogical theories determined their acceptance or rejection of computer use. They examined the *pedagogical value* of the technology before they were willing to invest time and other resources in developing it.

For these teachers, successful, long-term learning about uses of classroom technology was anchored in their definition of pedagogical problems. All the teachers used computers to address aspects of teaching they found challenging: for example, teaching students to write well, fostering higher order thinking skills, guiding students as they grasped scientific concepts in ways they would retain and could extend, integrating the computers themselves into their daily work in a business setting. Addressing such challenges, the computer-using teachers looked to technology as a possible solution.

With a pedagogical problem in mind, the teachers searched for possible solutions. At this point, the professional support that teachers received from the school and district became quite important. An open system, which supported the idea of new information coming into the school, and support for professional development that permitted and paid for teachers to attend conferences meant that teachers could search for solutions—technological or not—to classroom challenges in multiple arenas. They scanned the environment for solutions. That environment included personal resources (such as personal contacts), university courses, professional networks, the Internet, professional conferences, colleagues within the school and outside it, and magazines, professional publications, or television.

Teachers who already had some faith that new technologies might hold solutions for their work tended to consider technological possibilities the most seriously. They looked for software, hardware, curricula, and uses that might help them in their classrooms. Those who were more skeptical of, or opposed to, using technology in the classroom also considered technologically supported solutions, but tended to dismiss them more quickly, for reasons rooted in their pedagogical theories. Teachers who ended up using the computers first saw what they needed in a computer-based application, then set about the hard work of developing particular uses that fit with their courses, classrooms, students, and teaching styles. In developing these uses, they focused on the pedagogical problem they had defined.

Underlying any talk about "learning" to do something is the assumption that there is an identifiable skill or concept available to be learned. People learn, for example, to ride a bike, to add numbers, to read, to write an essay, to analyze data. However, examination of the learning of teachers in this study caused me to understand in different terms what it means to "learn" to use classroom technology. Since each curriculum, each teacher, and each group of students are different, teachers did not so much "learn" a particular use as create one particular to their own subject knowledge, pedagogical knowledge (Shulman, 1986), curriculum, and students. (This idea will be discussed and illustrated further below.) Indeed, the teachers here tailored their use of technologies in very specific ways; this process resembled a new *creation* more than a "learning" as they are commonly defined. For example, one teacher took word processing and adapted it to teach writing; two had students develop very different kinds of Web pages to demonstrate course learning; another adapted an existing curricular software package and added many pieces to it in a science classroom. None took a predeveloped piece of software or curriculum and put it in his or her classroom; "implementation" would be an entirely inappropriate word for this process.

This creation of new curriculum and practice, oriented toward solving a pedagogical problem, was the essence of these teachers' learning. It required that they have access to new ideas and that they be granted the flexibility by school administration and parents to try new classroom practice. But fundamentally, this new creation was what got meaningful uses of technology into their curricula and gave those uses both quality and staying power.

After creating uses they thought would work, often over summer or other vacations, the teachers took them to their classrooms. They tested new units, new assignments, new lessons, entirely new ways of teaching their curricula. Discussions with them following classroom observations about how they developed their work over time showed that they made adjustments at every opportunity. Sometimes large overhauls occurred from year to year, sometimes smaller ones. At times, they adjusted from class period to class period, tweaking lessons and uses over the course of a day, or a unit. Each one of the teachers refined their work over a period of years, during which they would develop better ways of teaching, more powerful ways of using the technology, new ways of assessing learning. This freedom to try new uses, reflect on them, and refine them over a period of years was critical to their learning and developing high-quality, appropriate uses of classroom technology.

I have described here an overall pattern into which the teachers' learning fit; each individual narrative will describe, in particular detail, how each teacher learned to work with instructional technology. It is important to notice both the fit within the pattern and the unique nature of each story, because, in the end, this study is about how individual learning, and ultimately the enactment of classroom practice, take place within an organizational and cultural context. In order to create organizations and policy contexts that promote teachers' learning, we need to understand the processes of that learning, and also how those individual processes are supported—or perhaps thwarted—by the school organization. This school and district succeeded by providing a combination of structure and flexibility, support and accountability, with professional autonomy within a strong pedagogical culture. Understanding the arc and logic of each teacher's learning and how it is expressed in practice is critical to grasping how this worked from the inside as well as the lessons that should be drawn from it.

The chapters that follow zoom in closely on the instructional practice and professional learning of five teachers, who were chosen because they all used computers for constructivist teaching, but taught different subjects, were involved with different academic departments, and used the computers somewhat differently. Their stories depict their work in the classroom and how they learned to do it, intertwining talk about technology, pedagogy, students, philosophies, and trial and error.

# CHAPTER 4

# Using Computers to Measure, Analyze, Model: The Physics Class

ROB TRACE began teaching physics at Woodland in 1981. After completing an undergraduate degree in psychology, he had become interested in teaching science as a career. He began working at WHS as a laboratory aide, then as a substitute, all while taking courses to obtain his teaching certificate. After a year at another high school nearby, a physics position opened up at WHS, and Rob returned there as a regular teacher.

From Rob's early work with students in the laboratory, he developed a strong sense of the power of hands-on learning, which clearly carried through to the classroom work I observed. From 1989 to 1994, he worked on and completed a master's degree in cognitive science and computers at a regional university and now teaches part-time in the same program. His master's work provided him with strong conceptual grounding in cognitive theory and its connections to instruction. For his master's thesis, he developed an interactive physics curriculum. This occurred around the same time the WHS school building was being renovated, and faculty were allowed input into the plans for the building. With the timing just right, he was able to set up a lab much like the one he had planned, and was provided the kind of technology he needed in the physical and architectural format he had designed. This coincidence of timing coupled with support from the school allowed him to pursue a unique and powerful instructional vision.

Rob's pedagogical approach was the most explicitly constructivist of the five teachers, both in its design and in terms of the language he used to talk about it. The physics class I observed was designed for students who were college-bound or already serious about learning physics, and who had sufficient background in mathematics. Rob cotaught this class with another teacher, David Brady. Along with several other teams in the Science Department, the two teachers coplanned and taught classes that had a larger number of students than those taught by a single teacher. I had hoped to include conversations with David in this study because he played an integral role in developing the instruction I will describe, but during 1997–98 he taught only part-time at WHS, which made it difficult to find sufficient time for interviewing. Below, I refer mostly to Rob's development of instructional ideas in the classroom because I was able to get his full story. However, it was clear that the two of them developed this challenging work as a team, and benefited from intensive interaction, sharing of ideas, and mutual goals for students.

## INSTRUCTION: A HANDS-ON APPROACH

Rob and David developed their first semester curriculum based on a series of lessons called RealTime, created by David Sokoloff, Ronald Thornton, and Priscilla Laws (1999), which would become a textbook in 1999. The lessons utilize probeware and software from several different sources to support students' explorations of physical concepts. During the first semester, the curriculum was structured through a series of labs, around which the teachers developed lectures, analytic sessions, theory-building exercises, and simulations. During the second semester of the course, there were some less interactive units, with a long-term independent research project due in the spring.

Structured by numerous activities, the class was tightly run; students were serious and busy. The classroom had lab benches with Macintosh computers around the perimeter—approximately one for every four students, so students generally worked in groups of four. Since the computer and attached peripherals were at the center of the lab activities, the members of each group shared data and worked together to analyze it.

During the first semester, in a series of units on motion, students explored physical phenomena by running experiments and collecting data. In the unit I observed most closely, students videotaped the movement of an object that had either constant velocity or constant acceleration. The movement of a cart or a dropping object was videotaped, then students used an application called VideoPoint to digitize a short section of the videotape. Calibrating the motion of the object against a ruler placed behind it produced data points for distance and a clock was used to measure the time.

Using the VideoPoint software, students were able to pull location and time data from the digitized video. They then used a piece of software called CricketGraph to chart the data, and inserted the appropriate formulas to calculate velocity and acceleration at each point. CricketGraph also allowed students to create graphs and charts. Students graphed velocity and acceleration, hypothesizing about the relationship between the two. Once they developed a theory about the relationship between these two variables, additional software packages allowed them to set up two kinds of simulations: a physical simulation and a systems simulation.

The students also used software that simulated their cart experiment as well as other experiments with collisions to test theories about the relationships among time, distance, velocity, acceleration, and force. Using the simulation software, they defined mathematical relationships between the variables, then were able to watch a simulation based on their model, showing what happened to velocity when they played with the time data, or to acceleration when they played with the velocity data. They were encouraged to play around with different settings to explore the response of the simulation.

Another application called STELLA, which was created at MIT for systems modeling, offered students an additional tool for exploring physical behavior. Students in this class used STELLA to describe how they understood causal and mathematical relationships between variables.

Students' labs consisted of all these components. Before they touched a piece of lab equipment, they were required to theorize about the relationship between velocity and acceleration. Throughout the course of the lab, which took 1 to 2 weeks of class time, they continually reviewed their theories. In the end, they represented their conception of motion through drawing pictures, recording raw data, creating graphs, producing mathematical equations, simulating the experiment on a computer, and developing a systems model to reflect it. Rob and David explained that they required all this from their students so that the learners produce multiple representations of the phenomenon under study. The teachers felt this process significantly deepened students' understanding and increased the percentage of students who would come to understand the topic. The laboratory-based instruction was supplemented with short lectures, readings, and sessions in problem solving.

Rob's pedagogical theory involved several principles. One was that students needed to construct their own knowledge, building on what they had before. When learning physics, Rob told me, students tend to have conceptions of the physical world that are intuitive but incorrect. Thus part of the challenge of teaching physics is to help students confront these misconceptions and understand relationships that are counterintuitive, but scientifically correct. Coaching students to build their own knowledge through hands-on lab work, analyzing data, and building theories about it, are all essential to this difficult learning.

When I asked Rob how he would describe to me his theory of teaching, he answered:

> It became a lot clearer to me through the process of doing my master's thesis: thinking about learning, not teaching. So it might be that a philosophy of learning is more appropriate. I think I'm mostly

a cognitive structuralist. . . . So I guess the way learning occurs, you have to have constructs that students can attach their stuff to—what they already know.

Rob and David had students develop theories about what might happen in a lab before trying it, a technique Rob picked up through his work with the American Association of Physics Teachers (AAPT).

A lot of what I know about precognition has come from AAPT conventions, hearing about misconceptions students have, which are rampant in the physical world. Because they have so much experience with the physical world, it's really hard to just teach them anything in physics without going through this. That's why we adopted the RealTime package because it forces them to confront their misconceptions: It creates discrepant events for them, and then they have to resolve them and reconstruct. So it's constructivist, but there's also a need to really link it to stuff they already know as much as possible.

Another critical component of his philosophy is that granting learners control boosts their engagement:

For their learning, part of the environment we create is one where they have a lot of control. I guess one way we do that is with their second-quarter project, where they can select whatever topic they're interested in. And we shape some of the goals such that it agrees with the physics curriculum, but they're in charge of the way it looks. So if they want to analyze motion in a clip from a film, or they want to do a soccer kick or whatever, they can. So they get invested in it that way.

This was balanced, however, with a sense that too much learner control means students may redirect their attention before facing the most difficult revisions in their thinking.

The problem with that was articulated to me by Tom Snyder. He gave us a lecture at MIT. . . . He really clarified it for me. He said that if you're watching TV, as soon as something gets a little too painful, you change the channel. And if kids have that kind of control—and that's a problem I see with multimedia tutorial type things—as soon as it gets a little bit too tough, a little bit uninteresting, they go to something different. And you never get to the point where you're learning anything—where you're really forced to change your stuff. And with this RealTime stuff, if kids could do that, as soon as they got to a point where their graphs didn't agree with what they believed, they'd go to something else, they'd study a different topic. They would never learn. So there has to be a definite structure and definite goals to it. But within that, you give them as much control as they can have, so they get choices.

He summarized his philosophy as follows:

> I think these are the pieces: keeping high standards. Keeping it tough for kids. High expectations, rather than lowering your standards because kids get frustrated. And just in terms of the profession, really having a love for kids and a love for your subject matter. Those are important pieces.

For Rob, the technology helped him accomplish the kind of teaching he wanted with more depth and at a higher level. The problem he posed for himself was how to provide a lab-centered curriculum during which students build their own knowledge and understanding of the physical world. Computers helped with data processing and provided tools for students to test out their understanding. They allowed the students to spend more time building and refining concepts and less time with pencil and graph paper. They helped the teachers combine elements of student control and independent learning with structure and a push toward high standards.

## PROFESSIONAL LEARNING: THEORY, INTENSIVE EXPERIENCE, CONTINUOUS IMPROVEMENT

Rob chronicled a series of experiences that contributed to his learning about how to use computers in the classroom. For example, during the early 1980s he and several others at the school participated in a technology-intensive program called the IBM Model Schools Project. A second important set of experiences was in connection with a collegial network, the American Association of Physics Teachers, through participating in a program designed to develop leading physics teachers nationwide. In 1994–95 Rob took a year's sabbatical to work at the Air Force Academy in an office developing technology-based curriculum materials. During that time, he learned about software development as well as about the organizational aspects of fostering technology use.

Like the other teachers in this study, Rob's grasp of how to use computers in the classroom evolved over the course of many years, beginning in the early 1980s. The nature of this exposure shaped his vision of how computers could be used as tools:

> In 1984, IBM started a project—the IBM Model Schools Project. . . .
> Five people were selected to go to the training for 3 or 4 weeks in the
> summer. . . . We were taught how to use regular tool software: word
> processing, databases, the IBM Filing Assistant series, their spread-
> sheet, and MultiPlan, the graphing assistant. The idea was to use
> those pieces of tool software, learn them, to figure out how to use
> them in the classroom. . . . So that concept of using tool software,
> and adapting it, because it was much more powerful, much more
> global—and training people in that, is something that's really stuck
> with me. So whenever I talk with anybody about educational technol-
> ogy, that's one of the tenets. You find a tool that's useful in a lot of
> ways and learn how to use it. You don't find one very specific
> program, unless it's really unique and you can't do it another way.

Rob believes in using the technology only when it augments what he's already trying to do in the classroom.

> That's really been a key piece of my philosophy. I mention this a lot
> when I teach my [college] course. You shouldn't just use technology
> because it's there. There are a lot of reasons to use it. With the
> technology you can do things that can't be done any other way—that
> can't be done easily, or that can't be done carefully. For example, all
> the RealTime stuff here, all the data capturing, the RealTime graph-
> ing. You can't do that with a stopwatch and a ruler. By the time the
> students get done producing the graph, they've forgotten what they
> did that made their graph look steeper than the other ones.
>     That's a positive use of technology. Something I think is not a
> good use is to have a kid browse the Internet. Unless they're trained
> in specific techniques so they can browse efficiently, they end up
> spending a lot of time looking around, and printing tons of stuff, and
> not being able to process it. So it's a very expensive use of resources,
> both time and hardware.

Back as far as 1984 then, Rob clearly perceived the value of using computers for teaching and developed some principles for how to use them. With this conviction, he moved forward to find various ways he could incorporate them, as tools, into his own teaching.

Over a period of years, Rob's knowledge and expertise using computers in the classroom has grown. He does not credit his background in psychology as being much help (too behavioristically oriented, he says), but it is clear that from early on he began figuring out how to apply the computers as classroom tools. Rob is a good example of someone who has used many resources over time to learn what he knows about using computers in the classroom. His technical expertise is especially high; I often saw other teachers turn to him for assistance or advice. One teacher told me, as she wheeled a computer into his classroom for him to take a look at, "You want to know how we learn about computers here? We ask Rob."

Rob outlined a combination of experiences that had shaped him as a teacher. In relating these events, he provided a narrative of his own development, illustrating the intertwining layers of technology and pedagogy.

> I think I could point back to several key incidents that really caused big leaps in my thinking as a teacher. The first one was, I had a year of lab aide experience, so I knew what labs were all about, and I graded labs, I did chemistry labs, and I knew that was fun to do for kids. So I started off with that type of approach rather than just talking all the time, or maybe having the kids in small group discussion all the time. I started from a lab mode, so that was just the onset.

Building from his start in the chemistry lab, the sequence of professional experiences Rob chose and the way he made sense of them helped him build a strong understanding of how computers could be used as tools in his field.

> I was taking courses all the time. You know, I would find a course and take it . . . something that was interesting. Around 1981 or 1982 I took a course at the state university on computers in math and science. We were using Commodore 64s. For my project, I wrote a BASIC program that performed a simulation. So you could plug in the mass of a planet and a radius. It would basically draw an ellipse for you. But you would change the variables, and the size of the ellipse would change. So you would ask a question, you know, about the effect of that. So then the kids would start with that kind of thing, where the computer was generating some data for them, that would then tie in, of course, to the study of orbits, or whatever we were studying at the time. I guess that was one of the areas that just came to mind quickly, but it was also an area that didn't have a lot of lab work that was real concrete. And I'd already realized at that point, that the abstract stuff was the real tough stuff, so you've got to make concrete activities for kids. So that was when I started to write programs and began to think about the computer as a simulation tool in the classroom.

Then in 1984 we had the IBM model schools project. As a result of participating in the project, I got a PC for my classroom. It was in the back of the room, and I would have each pair of kids or each kid go back there and, say, type their project into a database. Or in the lab rotation, one of the steps was to use a spreadsheet to develop theories about the source of error in a calorimetry lab: hot metal in cold water. . . . If you're off half a degree, it could change your answer by 15%. So using the spreadsheet that way let them pin down what a realistic source of error was.

Rob's next step was becoming involved in the American Association of Physics Teachers in 1985. This subject area network had a strong effect on Rob's development, providing opportunities to see other teachers at work, learn about new ideas and research in the field, and be exposed to new software and uses for computers. His singular story supports research on the power of professional networks for teacher learning (Darling-Hammond & McLaughlin, 1996). The focus on subject matter was particularly powerful, providing very specific, useful concepts, techniques, and lessons. He received intensive training as part of the AAPT's Physics Teachers Resource Agents (PTRA), a program designed to create a national network of highly skilled physics faculty.

We went out to Flagstaff, Arizona, for a 3-week training session. Twenty days straight of training—we got Father's Day off. We did Saturdays and Sundays, and all kinds of things. Every night there were demonstration shows. We all had to bring demonstrations, and we'd spend about an hour watching other people's demonstrations. Just seeing all those demonstrations opened my eyes to different ways you could do things.

I guess the critical piece for me at the PTRA sessions was that it linked me to the national organization and provided me with funding to go to the next three national meetings. So I was at the summer meeting the next couple years after that. Since then I've made a majority of those meetings.

Over the course of the PTRA program, those 300 teachers in the first 3 years are probably responsible for a large number of the innovations that have gone on in physics. But the contact is a real key. Because through the AAPT meetings, I would find stuff that was interesting to see. That's where I first saw digital video stuff. And I knew once I saw it that I had to have that. So I went right up to Priscilla Laws after the meeting and said, "I'd be interested in doing a test for you." And she said, "Well, stop by and see me tomorrow and

I'll give you a copy of the disk." So that's where we started with our digital video analysis. That really opened up worlds for us. In fact, we were still using that same software up to and including last year.

Rob went on to describe the beginning of his use of the RealTime curriculum in the classroom, and how he increasingly incorporated probeware to measure physical phenomena and transfer that data into a computer. The RealTime curriculum suited Rob's philosophy of interactive, hands-on work for students. At the same time, he found probeware developed by David Vernier which would measure motion (Vernier, 2004). He started out by making do with just one motion detector and one video station. The students would do a five-part lab, going from station to station.

At the same time, the new science wing was being built at WHS. This provided the opportunity to design a classroom environment that would suit the lab-based, computer-integrated approach. "I was interested in the lab, so it was a natural fit for me to get the stuff into the hands of the kids, rather than me using it as a presentation tool. I wasn't interested in a new filmstrip projector; I was interested in the kids doing work."

In 1994–95, Rob was offered a sabbatical to work with instructional technology at the Air Force Academy. Even though sabbaticals are provided for within the teachers union contract, few teachers actually get to take them, and administrators I spoke with admitted frankly that they use them to support the kind of work that they want to be visible and clearly valued, such as the use of technology. As such, it was an honor and mark of status to be awarded a sabbatical.

At the Air Force Academy, Rob worked on developing multimedia-based instructional materials and learned more about organizational factors that can support technology use. When he returned to WHS, he instituted a process by which teachers could request a budget for new computers and other technology. By describing their instructional purpose and defining what equipment they needed, teachers at WHS could request technology for the following year through the school's technology budget, managed by the Technology Committee. At the end of the 1997–98 school year, Rob accepted part-time work as the technology integration specialist for the school, in which role he would assist other teachers seeking to incorporate technology.

Over the years, Rob's teaching changed to assimilate new technologies. From what I observed and from what he told me, at every step this required many adjustments and changes. When a teacher has to create new lessons, new classroom routines, and new assessments, he is essentially creating new curriculum. As he did this, Rob remained true to his philosophy regarding the importance of laboratory work, and still uses today some of the techniques he used when he began. However, his theories about teaching and learning gradually changed. To understand the shift, I asked him what his classroom looked like before 1984, when he began using computers.

> A lot of labwork. A substantial amount of lecture, problem solving, where I would be giving them a problem and then walking around the room looking at things. Kids would do reports and presentations . . . and this is a while back. But there's always been a lot of laboratory work. I would set up a week's worth of labs, a whole bunch of different stations. This was particularly true in areas where I had a limited amount of equipment, or a lot of different subthemes, where you'd need to spend a whole period—and these were 40-minute periods at that time—on any particular topic. So they would come in and be working through all these things, and we'd analyze them and talk about them as a class, and they'd turn in lab reports and stuff like that. Then there'd be a problem-solving component generally as homework. We'd have a day where I'd be doing problems up on the board, and they'd be asking questions. I'd be giving them sample problems. Then there would be an introductory lecture.
>
>     I was backwards in my approach in that I'd tell them first what they should get out of the work, then give them the labs, then the problems, then test them at the end to see if they got it. So that's what it looked like. And then when I saw the RealTime lab curriculum I started to shift to the idea that students are building their knowledge, constructing it. And at the same time, some of the research in the physics teaching community, AJP, American Journal of Physics, was showing that students really weren't getting this stuff. Things like the Force Concept Inventory came out, and so we started looking for a different way to approach the teaching, so it became more constructivist.

Here, Rob demonstrates his thinking about why he has moved toward a more constructivist model over time. He knew that he had to pursue something different because results on classroom assessments that challenged students with a range of problems showed that they had achieved only limited understanding in many areas. For example,

> A lot of the kids had memorized Newton's third law. And as long as I told them this is a physics test, they'd get it right. If I set it up in different situations, they wouldn't. They didn't internalize it. So we made a specific shift [away from memorization and toward constructivism] as part of this program.

> But that whole shift necessitated dropping out some things. So lectures became very infrequent. Looking over lesson plans from years past, we used to spend a lot more time lecturing but now it's gone down to more like 10%.

Rob's reflection on how well students were learning was based on the results of various assessments he and David used. The results helped them determine how their teaching might be adjusted. Although Rob enjoyed doing demonstrations on PowerPoint or other software, he was skeptical about their teaching value, and so limited his use of them.

> I'm not convinced that demonstrations are effective teaching, even though I like them a lot. Because lots of times, I would choose a subtheme like fluid dynamics and set up an hour's worth of demonstrations on melting point, fluid dynamics, Bernoulli's principle, Pascal's . . . you know, a whole bunch of things. I would go through them with the students and talk about what they thought would happen, why it didn't happen, what was going on. And then, 3 days later, I'd give them a test and say, "Choose one of the following and explain it." I got very, very poor results. So, I like demonstrations, but I don't see them as very effective.

During my observations of Rob and David's classes during 1997–98, I observed the teachers' continued reflection. For each lab in the first semester, students received packets of written instructions. Rob and David kept a master packet, on which they recorded any necessary changes in instructions or technique for the next year. David conducted a survey with students asking them which elements of the labs they felt worked best for them. The results of each lab and exam the students took were analyzed, and at the end of the semester the two teachers were concerned that, according to results on the final exam, the girls in the class seemed to be learning the computer skills less well. I watched as their instruction was continually refined based on their observations of students and evidence from their assessments. They did this very intensely, partly because of their need to plan and execute the class together, and partly because of their reflective habits. This cycle of trying, reflecting, and refining was continually enacted over the course of years, semesters, months, weeks, and days, to adjust pieces of instruction as needed. The process formed a critical, ongoing piece of the teachers' learning and re-creation of curriculum and instruction.

# CHAPTER 5

# Strengthening Interdisciplinary and Multidimensional Understanding: Ancient Greek Language, History, and Literature

PETER MARCAZ is easily one of the school's most vocal and charismatic teachers. When other teachers listed the most influential faculty in the school, they mentioned his name more often than any other. Peter began teaching at Woodland 15 years ago, following a stint as education director at a local museum nationally known for its collection of American folk art. Prior to working as an educator, he was a playwright who undertook a range of jobs to support his writing. He has many skills and wide-ranging knowledge, describing himself as "almost omnivorous when it comes to learning."

Peter's vision of education includes using computers and the Internet as an "alternative delivery system" for schools. He believes, for example, that a teacher could place assignments on a Web page and then support students' independent work by offering them the appropriate resources as they work their way through a project. He feels that when they publish their work on a Web site, they experience what it means to have a public audience. He holds a broad pedagogical vision of creating a classroom in which curriculum is strongly interdisciplinary and students are highly motivated, independent learners. His vision is that his students should behave as—and think like—scholars.

## INSTRUCTION: MOTIVATION, SEQUENCING, DEPTH

The course Peter developed and named Ancient Greece and You was in its second year when I arrived at WHS. Peter developed the course after enrolling in a summer session at Tufts University, followed by a study sabbatical during 1995–96. At Tufts he studied Greek language, history, and literature, and worked with the Perseus Project, a rich, hyperlinked, multimedia database on the history and culture of ancient Greece (Tufts University, 2003). These experiences inspired Peter to develop a course for his high school students that would take an interdisciplinary approach to classics: teaching Greek language, literature, and history together, affording depth to students' understanding of the classics. Enrolled students could choose to receive foreign language credit, English credit, or social studies credit for their completion of the course. This created a very complex and rich course of study, but it also required Peter to prepare for three courses within this one, in addition to his other teaching responsibilities.

Peter developed the curriculum for the course based on Bloom's taxonomy of educational objectives, which recommends that teachers begin by teaching knowledge of facts, then help students use the knowledge base to develop higher order thinking skills (Bloom, 1956). Guided by Bloom's theory, Peter spent the first part of the yearlong course providing students with information about the history and culture of Greece. He felt the information was essential if the students were to move to higher level thinking later in the year. He characterized this first part of his curriculum as "almost a regular course."

Peter believed that the information obtained during the fall semester of the course would enable students to work more independently during the winter and spring to explore topics of their choosing. Topics they were allowed to elect fell within conceptual categories defined by Peter, such as politics, economics, or culture. Within each of these topics, Peter developed a range of assignments that would move students through increasingly complex levels of knowledge in preparation for a particular project. Students also proposed their own projects on occasion. Peter allowed them to pursue their own idea as long as they could describe its importance and how they would demonstrate their knowledge of it.

Of the five case study teachers, Peter was the one wandering farthest out on the edge of his own learning during the year I spent at Woodland. With a new curriculum and a broad vision of how to use technology, he was pushing the envelope conceptually and technically. For example, I watched as he learned to conceive and execute Web page development at the same time his students were undertaking their own Web page assignments.

Peter's philosophy of teaching was that students must be motivated to learn or no learning can occur. He attempted to build their motivation by combining tough grading, charisma, interesting material, and a humorous but tough sort of badgering.

My basic philosophy is if they are not awake they can't learn. And everything else is secondary. I'll do what I can to stimulate them to be awake. If it's insulting, I'll insult them. If it's entertain them, I'll entertain them. It doesn't really matter, but I'm excited about the subject matter. It's exciting. It's just plain exciting. I think that students have had so many poor experiences with learning, with teachers who are bored with their subject matter or don't know very much about it, or both, that the excitement is stimulating to them in itself. And so I try and do that and sometimes it works and sometimes it doesn't. But I know that the better prepared I am, the better they have a chance to learn.

Peter's emphasis on motivating students was backed by his own passion for the subjects he taught. I sensed that he wished to convey that love of literature, history, and language, to help his students become genuine scholars of the classical age, even if briefly. He believed students should develop a love for learning, and hoped that with his guidance, and some discipline, students would discover some of the joys of intellectual pursuit.

One of the reasons I have multiple certifications and broad knowledge is because it doesn't work any other way. It doesn't make sense to me any other way. Literature doesn't make any sense to me without history, and it doesn't make any sense to me without language. And I would hope that at least the first steps for students trying to link these things together for themselves makes them come to the same conclusion. I'm not really sure that there's any true learning that takes place that's not heuristic. That may not be the case, but I know that heuristic learning is *some* of the best learning, if not *the* best. . . .
    By this I mean discovery learning. They have a need for something or they discover something, and they say, "Aha!" that type of a thing. . . . Giving them an opportunity to manipulate information and come to that heuristic spot is better, I think, than any other type of learning. . . . But the hard thing, especially in high school, is that if you believe in heuristic education, you always have to draw back, and set aside time, and allow them to discover things.

I asked Peter how this philosophy played out in the way he designed his course curriculum and daily instruction. He showed me grids on a variety of topics with assignments that move students from knowledge through to analysis and application, in the way of Bloom's taxonomy. He believes in the kind of rigor rooted in a strong knowledge base that leads students to investigate thoughtful questions.

You have to have enough tools to be able to manipulate to make your own creation. If you don't have enough [intellectual] tools, you can't make your own creation, and all you're doing is basically moving the same three or five things around. And so grammar schools that don't teach math facts, grammar, and all of those things because they are afraid of [lowering] the self-esteem of the kid, I think they have it exactly backward. Because the self-esteem of the kid is raised when they do something well, and they know it, and false praise doesn't do anything. . . .

The tension in this class is the same thing. I want them to understand Plato so that they can start playing with language, and so they can start thinking philosophically. But to understand Plato really takes a lot of basic knowledge. "What's a fortiori reasoning? What's happening in this particular area? What's he doing here? He is setting up a false analogy." That's all new stuff in the same way that multiplication tables are new to a second grader. That's what I try and do the first quarter, quarter-and-a-half—give them all the tools necessary so that when they go out and play, they can do something. And that's the struggle between content and process so to speak. . . . How do I get them ready to play with it independently, without spending a whole year or 2 years or 3 years teaching? And so that's the tension in this class.

The format of Peter's class varied a great deal, depending on the topic, the prior knowledge of the students, which group of students (English, social studies, Greek language) were required to be in class, and what projects were being worked on at the time. Peter held lecture and discussion on some days, and time for work on group projects other days. Students reporting to this first-period class at 8 A.M. generally saw a schedule posted on the door. During the second semester, when he had the literature, history, and Greek language groups in one course, he alternated meeting with the different groups of students, often splitting 90-minute blocks into two segments. Those who were not in class were required to work independently on their projects during class time.

Peter's commitment to integrating computers into classroom life was very strong, evidenced by his continuing efforts to learn about the possibilities of the technology as well as his attempts in the classroom. As students developed their research projects that spring, Peter at first suggested, then for a later project required, that they create Web pages that would present the research to the class. Peter used the hyperlinked nature of Web design to facilitate depth and breadth in the research process, to promote students' thinking about how their work linked to other topics, authors, and ideas, and to provide a format for a wider audience than the traditional research paper. Peter accepted that his students would build their technical facility as they went along—and that he would strengthen his own knowledge alongside them.

Peter linked computer use directly to his vision of education. I asked him why he used computers at all—what, in his opinion, made using them better than not doing so.

> I think the jury is still out on that. Obviously the ability to access huge amounts of information is an important reason, otherwise why bother with this? I mean to get on the Vatican Library [site], and see [original documents] is thrilling. That's the obvious reason. But at what stage should you be doing this, and what does it replace? . . .
>
> You only have 6 hours a day with the kids. And if you do this, you replace what you were doing previously. And the thing that you're not doing here is some disciplined book learning. And exactly how is using the computers more effective than that? . . .
>
> If you're using this tool as a teaching tool, as a demonstration tool, as a hyperlink tool and everything else, I think the learning that takes place is transferable into some things that they will be learning later in life. That's a guess.

I asked him how he thought asking students to produce a Web page was different or better than having them write a paper. In his answer, he conveyed his conception of how creating a Web page can be a powerful learning experience, quite distinct from producing a traditional research paper. The process differs, he argued, as does the audience for the piece.

> They have to write in order to do a Web page. But they also have to—in a kinesthetic fashion, if you want to go into Gardner's multiple intelligences—highlight the links and do more than just write it down. They have to put in the link, and by playing on that, I think they start seeing a three-dimensional concept, rather than a two-dimensional concept. That is something different than the student thinking, "Here's another paper. I've been doing these papers my whole 12 years, and I could move these out in my sleep."

Making a Web page, Peter argued, requires the students to think more broadly and allows them to discover aspects of their topic facilitated by the many linkages of the World Wide Web: "One of the goals of the course is to have them see things that they have never seen before. Some of these links are taking them places that they wouldn't have investigated ordinarily."

Many students who chose a topic would begin with a superficial exploration, then move through various levels to explore more deeply, which Peter described as a "multitiered experience." That the students chose their own topics, and were able to research them as they chose, created both a deep, linked experience, and one that was intrinsically motivating:

> I think we give a lot of lip service to intrinsic motivation for learning, while we practice extrinsic motivation of learning. And those two have never really found a common ground before. And this tends to turn into—or can turn into—where through an extrinsic assignment, students all of a sudden start learning intrinsically because they go places that aren't teacher-directed places, they are student-directed places. And it's fun. It's just plain fun. And we don't know where the student is going to end up.

## PROFESSIONAL LEARNING: UNIVERSITY-BASED, SELF-TAUGHT, RELYING ON STUDENTS

Peter began using computers in the classroom in the mid-1980s with a classroom full of Apple IIs and a popular program called Bank Street Writer. He took over the school's yearbook in 1988 to use the computers for simple layout, and expanded his use of them each year thereafter. He began using e-mail in the early 1990s, and shortly after set up a program for his students to correspond electronically with residents of a local retirement home. Peter created new classroom practices by being exposed to a technological application, teaching himself more about it, then creating new uses for the classroom.

Peter developed an interest in hyperlinked databases when he discovered the Perseus Project (now called the Perseus Digital Library; see Tufts, 2003). In the mid-1990s, Perseus produced a HyperCard database of classics materials that was available on CD. Users were able to annotate the available information by creating "trails" through the program. At first, upon returning from his sabbatical at Tufts, Peter tried to use the Perseus program, but found it unwieldy. He experimented with linking the database to HyperCard programs, but did not find that worked well either. He eventually found that having students create a Web page would accomplish much the same thing, because they would have to read about a topic, then organize it according to conceptual categories they generated themselves. This skipped the annotation, but was a product that required students to read extensively and present their findings in a way that emphasized conceptual interconnections.

The year I observed was the first year Peter actively worked on Web site development with students, and he was busy as well developing his own course Web site. When I asked him how he was learning about Web site development, he responded that with this, like other applications he has learned, he studies it on his own, using manuals, through trial and error. He told me that he occasionally asks other adults for help, but more often leverages the expertise of students.

From observing Peter's learning over the course of the year, I found his characterization true. He was willing to jump right in and try new software, and willing to withstand the early confusion of the process, knowing that eventually he would learn it. Indeed, the progress he made learning to develop new Web sites and teaching students how to do it between December and June was remarkable.

Peter's method for learning a new technology was to choose a promising application and run with it. He jumped right into using it in the classroom. He described the process as "just stumble and fall." He drew upon text resources, online help, occasional persons, and his own persistence.

During the semester, Peter also experimented with putting homework assignments on the Web and having students check there each evening. Doing so required a change in habits for the students, which they resisted somewhat. This experiment faded after a while, probably because it was difficult for Peter to keep up with posting the assignments and because a significant number of students resisted checking the site each day. However, over the year he also posted resources for students on the Web, such as links to the Perseus Project and other sites with information on Greek classical literature or history. This technique developed quite nicely over the course of the year, and I observed students using these resources frequently during their research.

Because Peter was teaching his new course for only the second time, in addition to integrating Web-based research and Web page production, he was creating new curriculum and instructional activities over the course of the semester I observed this class. While he had designed the backbone of the curriculum—topics to be covered and the categories in which students would do projects—the actual lessons were often new.

For the first project students did that year, creating the Web page was optional. But what unfolded underlined the benefits from Peter's perspective:

> For writing teachers, the problem that we always run into is audience—that you need to write for your audience. And for 12 years these students have written for an audience of one, which is the teacher. . . . For instance, there were two different English groups that I assigned to read Aristophanes. And they had to present what they thought about it to the class. In addition to presenting, one group also made this Web page with links and all kinds of stuff. And the

other group said, "Oh! That's really neat. We didn't do that." It makes a big difference in how they look at each other and how they are perceived by their peers. In the philosophy Web pages [that the students produced], the page on beauty was redone at least four or five times as the student started seeing other people's pages. After they saw some of the other pages, between the five groups there started to be a little bit of competition.

After some of the initial presentations, students asked Peter if they could have more time to polish their projects. During this time, they presented their work as drafts and accepted feedback from other students.

It was public, but it was also different than giving a presentation, where the students stand up in front and all their friends support them. This was public and yet it was divorced from that. So all the rest of the students were able to look at it with a more honest eye. They said "Hey, you could have done this. You could have done that."

Since Peter was so actively creating new uses during the year I observed, I had many opportunities to ask him to reflect on his innovations. His words illustrate how he thinks about the strengths and weaknesses of what he'd done in the classroom, his reflective process, and what he planned to change in the future. This case, in particular, illustrates the critical importance of teachers feeling free to take risks in the classroom, reflect upon, and refine their work without penalty. This process was at the center of Peter's learning experience, and facilitating it was the critical role of the school organization.

The second project during the spring semester dealt with philosophical topics. Students read, attempted to understand, and wrote about such topics as love, death, beauty, and the cosmos. Students wrote pieces expressing their understanding of the idea, published them on a Web page, and in most cases created links within the piece that provided more information on a philosopher or concept. Peter found that presenting their work to the class and posting it on the class Web site raised the stakes for students. They seemed to take their work more seriously.

I asked Peter on several different occasions how he planned to assess the students' work creating Web pages. What would make a good Web page to him? What characteristics would it have? He struggled with this question because although he had a sense that creating hyperlinked Web pages would be a powerful experience for students, he hadn't done it in the classroom enough to figure out exactly what a good page or site should look like. The following is an extract from one of our conversations, showing his reflective process on the work students produced and what might make it better. Here, we were talking specifically about the philosophical assignment just described.

> How to assess the work has been hard, as you know, to decide. There are three things that I ended up looking at. One of them was the text that's written. Did they take that information from the six pages of the *Encyclopedia of Philosophy*, and digest it, and understand it, and then put it into readable terms for their peers? I thought they did well with that. They really worked hard on it. . . . So the first question is, Were they able to do the assignment? The second one is, Did they put in enough links? Did they put in the links so that someone reading the paper, who wanted to go into more depth, could follow those links into better depth? Or did they just include the first things that came up?
>
> The third is, What is the reason for the link? It should substantiate what is going on within the paper. And there were some good links, and there were some bad links. Some of the links ended up of less quality than I would have liked. For example, they did a search for Schopenhauer, and they took the first link off of the search page and put it in there, and that was it. It ended up being somebody's biography of him. It had nothing to do with his philosophy.
>
> This one [showing me an example] is nice because they have a biography here, and then they have the philosophy here. I didn't have them defend why they chose their links, but we did talk about what makes a good link. And I gave some examples of good and bad links. Here's another one, a poorer example, here in the Socratic definitions, in a page on beauty. Now this really doesn't have that much to do with beauty—nothing to do with Socrates' concept of beauty—so it's not as good.

I asked Peter if he thought anything had changed in his approach to the Web page assignment or the students' approach between the first project and the second project, the philosophy page.

> I think the first was more like a published paper. A paper that they just published on the Internet. Whereas with the second set they started to explore what a hypertext paper could be. Of course, some explored it more than others.
>
> [Showing me a page.] This paper here was designed as a hypertext paper, I think. Now I would have liked—and I talked

about this with the students—to have a little bit more text here. But you can see that, compared to the others, it was written more with the links in mind.

As Peter evolved his conceptualization of the assignment and developed his ability to describe it for students, the students had to think more carefully about how they would construct the page to relate pieces of information to one another. In describing this evolution, Peter described the first phase as writing a research paper, posting it to the Web, and seeing what links are available to add. It was a process that just fancied-up a research paper. But when students developed a Web site from their research and included their original writing, they had to consider the structure of information and the links between it. This was what Peter was working toward that semester.

I asked him if and how his teaching differed between the first project and the second project of the semester.

> I got out of the way more. In the first one, I gave them the Bloom's taxonomy I'd developed for their topic areas. And I said, "Okay. When you finish this, I want you to present at least part of it on the Web." And so I ended up getting a lot of written papers that were transferred onto the Web. In the second one, I gave them an article from the *Encyclopedia of Philosophy*, and said, "[Think through] this, work over this with your partner. Figure out what it means, and then present that meaning on the Web, so that other people can understand it and have the links and everything like that." In the first project, they could have approached it any way that they wanted to. By the time we hit the second assignment, I had also grown, and was able to guide them better, because I had been making up [my own] Web pages, and running into problems there.

Finally, I asked what he would plan to do differently with the next project, which he would assign at the end of the year. He said he would like to see the pages better designed, so the reader would understand where he or she is on the page at any given moment, and went on to say:

> I'm going to be much more strict about the integration. Working with them on having a three-dimensional integration. [I'm going to ask the students to consider:] "Is there something here that a normal person would need more information about? How should they gain that information: by you telling them, or by them going somewhere else and seeing what other people have written about it? Why are you

duplicating work that's already done?" And so I think we're going to be working a lot more on the three-dimensional hypertext idea, as opposed to just a flat text.

Peter continued to work on the many dimensions of his vision that semester and planned more Web-based work for the following years. Using the base he had developed, and through trial and error, he continued to develop his use of Internet databases, Web research, and Web page design to augment his teaching.

# CHAPTER 6

# Simulating the Real World: Modern Economics

JOEL GREENE, who taught economics, was the most experienced of the five teachers described here; 1997–98 was his 29th year at WHS. With a strong background in his subject area, he easily adopted the role of expert in the classroom. His pedagogical philosophy focused on introducing students to concepts in economics, then creating activities in which they acted out practical applications for the same concepts. His goal was to reach as wide a range of students as possible, from those highly academically oriented to those less so.

In Joel's economics classes, he combined a relaxed stance with a deep, rigorous, and confident knowledge of economics, business, and finance. Like all of WHS's teachers, he was highly responsive to students, replying to questions and concerns during class and outside of it. Students who were strongly interested in business were drawn to him; they used him as a resource and sometime financial advisor.

As Joel told me about his background, he emphasized that he "came from a business family—a lot of people involved in business." After obtaining a 2-year business degree, he completed a 4-year program in education, followed by an MBA specializing in finance. He learned to use computers gradually over the years, beginning with programming on mainframes in the early 1980s and progressing to the PCs of the present day. He used computers for instruction wherever possible, but felt the technology had only recently developed sufficiently to make it really useful for teaching. For his work, he needed flexible space and time, fast, reliable Internet connections, and the ability to simulate real-world problems as they occur in business and economics.

## INSTRUCTION: "KNOWING WHEN SOMEONE IS TRYING TO DO YOU IN"

Joel assigned a wide variety of projects that required students' active participation. I observed units in two of Joel's economics classes over the course of the spring semester. Desks in his classroom either faced front or were arranged in groups, depending on the planned activities for the day. There was one computer, quite old, in the back of this classroom. I never saw it used, though Joel told me it was from time to time. Rather, students accessed computers in other spaces such as the library or social studies lab.

Joel created a climate in the classroom that linked students minute by minute to happenings in the business world. On the upper left-hand wall of his room, a television tuned to one of the financial cable channels provided constant updates on the stock market and business news, generating a sense of continuous connection to the financial world. During class, Joel would comment on the news, adding information and offering analysis. To complement this, he provided printed resources for students, including books on different industrial or financial sectors, companies, and stocks, along with daily newspapers.

Joel combined a variety of instructional approaches: short lectures, research papers, simulations, and projects. Students had a textbook for reference, but seemed to get most of their information from handouts, short lectures, research projects, other students' research presentations, and by questioning Joel directly. The conceptual basis for a unit, once laid, was capped by a longer term project that students would undertake individually or in small groups. The project usually involved research, problem solving, a thought experiment (what would you do if . . . ?), or a complex simulation.

In one exercise, students were given portfolios of $20,000 of pretend money. They were assigned to use this currency to buy and sell stocks, at their actual and current market price, over a period of months. Joel anchored the simulation with short lectures on such topics as how to understand the market position of a business, how to read a prospectus, the rise and fall of stock prices, and the role of options and futures. Joel directed students to the newspaper, television, or the Internet to obtain current prices and information on specific companies. The television in the classroom served as a virtual ticker tape, with stock prices running on the bottom, and occasional news flashes about a particular stock or business sector. Often quite concerned about their portfolios, students would stop to comment on an investment they'd made, or Joel might point up a bit of breaking news to discuss its significance.

When it came time to work directly on their portfolios, several students remained in the classroom to use the newspapers, books, or other resources Joel had provided, but most students split off to one of the places that had computers available. They went over to a room called the social studies lab with 8 new computers, or they headed down to the library, which had an open lab with 16 computers for student use. During one class, Joel suggested a Web site where students could track stock prices, but a student suggested an alternative site which the students liked better and quickly adopted. For Joel, this was not a problem, but rather a positive experience for the students in finding and sharing resources. On this particular site, students could obtain the price history of any stock, and could input their investment choices and track them over time. Many students began using the site as a primary resource for tracking their gains and losses. A group of students in the social studies lab, without the urging or presence of the teacher, talked with one another about how to understand the historical graphs and how to obtain further information on the company through the site. They celebrated their gains and mourned their losses, as people do in any competition.

Joel circulated through the spaces where students were working, answering questions and making comments on various investments or stocks. With his extraordinary knowledge of the field, he was easily able to answer the many questions put by students. A few approached the class perfunctorily, but many others had discovered that they could get a wealth of information from Joel, and would pursue him with lots of questions during class, before and after class, in his office, and in the hallways.

Another exercise, which Joel ran for the entire semester, involved a computer-simulated resource game called Feudal Lords, set in medieval England. Teams of students were each given a fief to rule, with a supply of money (gold) and labor (peasants). For each turn of the game, the teams made strategic decisions about their labor supply, trading, and political and military plans. Students could opt to invade a neighboring fief or create alliances with its government, all with the purpose of making their kingdom stronger. During each class the game was played, they worked in teams to decide and negotiate, then submitted sheets detailing their decisions. Each turn, every 2 to 3 weeks, was mailed to a company in Arizona. There, the sheets were run through a computer program that combined all the decisions to provide each team with their status for the next round. This resource allocation game simulated the combined effects of economic and political decisions, as well as the complexity introduced by externalities. The students eagerly anticipated the day when the computer-generated results would come in the mail, so much so that the main office secretary had to hide the mail from Arizona until she could get it to Joel. The game would continue all semester or until one group was crowned ruler of all the land.

Another activity, which Joel explained to me but I was not able to observe, simulated the Federal Reserve System. One person would play secretary of the treasury, and students were allowed to take out loans and make investments. They could see interest rates rise and fall, and begin to understand the impact of government-determined interest rates on the economy.

Joel's philosophy was that students learn best through assignments where they could try out abstract ideas in a realistic situation. He found simulations worked especially well for him. Simulations require students to exercise newly learned skills and knowledge, but their outcomes are neither predictable nor determined by the teacher. Joel felt that for students, owning and controlling their own work was of primary importance; they must be truly engaged with the project and learn from their own mistakes. He felt the active learning and student control afforded by simulations were the best way to create this for students:

> In all these simulations that I've done, whether they're computer simulations or we run a full economy in the classroom with fake money and the whole thing . . . everything is there for them to learn and do and they have to work to learn it. They have to learn by doing it, whether it's in the markets or whether it's in the Federal Reserve game that I play. So . . . it's giving them the power and the control. What I like about it is that the students can make whatever they can out of it. Like Feudal Lords. They make what they make out of that by their own mistakes and their own successes. That's a real learning experience, I think, other than just being told about ideas and concepts.

The simulations, with their real-life feel, motivated students, but they also altered the teacher's role:

> As soon as [the students] believe it's not a sham, that they're in control, they really take off. And I guess that's why the course has been so successful here, because the kids know they can do it themselves and I'll be a consultant. And I'll give them my experience and background and whatever, but ultimately they make the decisions and I don't tell them what to do. I guess that's the philosophy I've always had. I mean, yeah, you've got to have the basics and I usually give them outline sheets and terms, or background material, but they won't really understand it until they really do something with it. They learn best by taking ownership of material. They learn best by doing what we talk about in some real way. That's what happens with the stock market game. They learn a lot more from this stuff than they would learn from listening to me. They can think they know the framework but then they lose money. Then they'll quickly understand what happens.

Joel valued the complexity simulations offer and that through them he could emphasize social learning in addition to the economic concepts. In the Feudal Lords simulation, for example, students work in groups. Teams have to negotiate with other teams to forge alliances that could ultimately conquer the kingdom. The individuals governing each fief had to work together to strategize ways to build, defend, and expand its dominion. This meant that students were involved in social and political interactions that Joel believed were vital for learning about economics and business. He emphasized that although computers were very important components of his classroom, it was extremely important that his students learn how to negotiate for business in the social world. Talking about the Feudal Lords simulation, he described how the computer became a tool for that process:

> It takes a big machine to run that thing, but they're not involved with the machine really. They're involved with the struggle, rather than just sitting at a terminal and playing some game. My students really like that combination of using a computer and the interaction between the different fiefdoms in a classroom. [Using] just the computer systems alone—I think that's a big mistake. I mean, you can put people in front of machines all day long and they could probably learn something, but they don't learn much about the interaction between people, which is the main part of what we do as humans on this planet. With some of the software for classrooms, the students just sit down and program. That's OK, and they may learn some of the facts and stuff. But they won't learn how to deal with another person who's trying to do them in, for example. Find out when somebody's lying to you and stuff like that. The real-world stuff. And that's the nice blend that game provides. It's like a reflection of life, and business, and everything rolled into one. You know, they can work as allies with other people and make a plan way ahead. They can make a lot of mistakes. But they usually learn from the mistakes they make—what happened, why. If they starve off half their peasants, there's a reason that happened. They made a big mistake. And then you look at the results like you do in the real world. You consider what happened and then you make some new decisions.

The key element of Joel's pedagogical philosophy is that students learn best by beginning with concepts and then applying them to complex, hands-on activities. The outcome should be real in the sense that their actions determine it, and there should be a wide variety of variables involved, simulating what they would find in the world of business. This pedagogical philosophy shaped how Joel chose to use computers to take advantage of the instant availability of information and complex simulations computers make possible.

Joel gradually incorporated computers into his teaching to fit this pedagogical theory. He developed his vision years ago, but found the technology inadequate to meet it. Only more recently was he willing to integrate computers fully with teaching, when he decided that they would not create more difficulties in the classroom than they solved. When the computer technology advanced sufficiently, his sense of the "relative advantage" (Rogers, 1995) of using computers tipped in the positive direction. First, they had to become accessible enough and fast enough to be smoothly and beneficially added to the classroom.

Describing this process, he told me:

> This is really the first time we've been able to use this technology in the classroom for something productive, other than just to make the school look good. The technology's been updated. I didn't really start using computers in the classroom until probably 5 or 6 years ago when we had enough machines for kids to sit down and use. And they were friendly enough for every student to use them. And we're getting to there now but we didn't get there for a long time. I've done everything mostly without computers in economics because there wasn't the capacity on the Internet up until 5 or 6 years ago to use for this. . . .
>
> In the early days the Internet was so unreliable I couldn't use it. But now you can. It would have been unmanageable 10 years ago because of the slowness of the system and the complexity of using it, the lack of resources. The first stuff was lousy. You probably remember the first Internet stuff was pretty bad. Now the quality has just increased dramatically. So I think that using the Internet tool is probably the greatest advantage that I have now. I want to do more of it.

Joel also believed that using computers the way he did created opportunities for a wider range of students to grasp the material, because it helped improve motivation and focus and made the content seem more relevant. It was important to him to make the economics course accessible to more than just the most academically oriented students, such as Advanced Placement or honors level.

> There are very smart kids who do this stuff without even taking a second breath. But the average kids need some reinforcement. And this course has to be some fun, too, because it's an elective course. I mean, I could make it the driest, most boring class in the building, if I taught traditional, classical economics. I'd have about three kids sitting up there. There've been a few of those. They read the book and learn the material. But that doesn't always mean they can cut the

best deal in the room. There are a lot of factors that go into the kind of multilevel thinking that goes on in reviewing, say, a business situation. You're dealing in a few words with other teams. It's interpersonal skills. [In a simulation], everything comes into play, like it does in the real world.

## PROFESSIONAL LEARNING: WAITING FOR TECHNOLOGY TO MEET THE NEED

Joel learned to use computers over many years, by employing a great variety of resources. He began using computers when they first became available during the mid-1970s, teaching programming and data processing at WHS by using punch cards on a computer with 20,000 bytes of memory. It wasn't until the mid-80s that computers began to be available for the classroom at WHS. At that time, "there were classes in math and in computers but there really wasn't any usage of them in other areas, curriculum areas and so forth. It just wasn't practical." The first technology he found effective for teaching in another subject area became available in the late 1980s. It was a system called Express which was "like a cable feed with information fed into a computer." Express provided a continuous stream of information such as news stories and stock prices. The access point to it was in the superintendent's office across the parking lot; it was the people in that office who told Joel about it and arranged for him to use it. He said that for a few years "it provided an updated version of the world in the classroom—something we now take for granted."

He began learning the Internet early in its existence and recalls the experience in a way that will be familiar to anyone who used it at that time. "When I started, it was really awful and slow initially. Nothing on there. Very little. The first system I used was Mosaic." I asked if he picked this up in conjunction with a group of people, but he replied that he learned it "on his own." People often use this phrase when describing how they learned computers, so I explored the idea further.

Joel described his learning about computers as something that occurred gradually, over a long period of time. He had a basis in mathematics and programming, but most of the rest occurred through independent learning. Like the other teachers in this study, Joel possessed a general enthusiasm for learning new things. In the discussion of organizational culture that comes later in this book, I argue that entry to the WHS organization (getting hired as a teacher), maintaining employment there, and conforming to everyday norms required that teachers be continuous learners. Joel fit this characterization well:

I'm real curious. I'm always watching. If there's a hi-tech show about computers on something like the Discovery Channel—I watch those shows all the time. I think that's where I get a lot of my information. The hard-core books, no I don't. Magazines, and if there's a good series on TV. When I started using the Web, at the very first, I used Jones [their former technical assistant] a lot. I was always talking to him about this stuff. I guess he and our assistant superintendent are always on top of it. So, I guess the other source is people. I don't necessarily read the magazines, the trades too much. But when I saw something that I could see would fit, I could see the potential of the Internet, even though it wasn't here for a while. Even though it wasn't powerful enough to [use a lot in the classroom], I could see unlimited possibilities for that. So I guess it would be . . . just my general curiosity with the stuff. I always like to know what's new, what's happening.

Joel took advantage of the leadership of the district on technology development, attending workshops and taking advantage of opportunities like the Express project. On technical issues, Joel would ask someone to show him how to use new software or hardware, drawing upon the school's infrastructure for technical support, especially the support personnel. He also described how he would teach himself:

[I think you need] the ability to sit down and play with something for a while. You have to do that with all this stuff. All these Internet sites. I'm getting so I have a pretty good repertoire of sites. I know pretty much where to send kids now. I'm self-motivated, I guess, on this stuff. And I go and search out help when I need it, if I'm really stuck.

I asked Joel specifically if he learned much from teachers at the same school or at other schools, but he returned again to the idea of teaching himself:

Self-learning, really. That's actually true for a lot of computer types who get into this stuff. I guess the curiosity is what drives you on. And you start to know how the stuff works or how you use it.

Although other teachers also said they taught themselves to some degree, for Joel it was his central form of learning.

In recent years, more and more of Joel's teaching has been constructed around integrating the computers in some way. Since the availability and efficiency of computers increased, he has changed many lessons and units to take advantage of the technology. The portfolio simulation I observed was done almost wholly on the Internet, whereas he had previously relied more on print materials and television. He ran the simulation on the Federal Reserve by combining a preprogrammed game he found and a computer program a student wrote to simulate the system. None of these pieces of Joel's curriculum was written for him; he created them. Even the Feudal Lords exercise, which is a game run on a remote mainframe, requires Joel to set the classroom context so that the students practice key concepts. It was what he wrapped around it—ideas about resource competition, planning, making and breaking alliances, cutting deals—that made Feudal Lords a powerful element of the economics curriculum.

Joel built his instructional practice by taking concepts of economics and business from a more general curriculum framework and developing units consisting of projects and simulations designed to challenge students and complexify their understanding. This is an example of how a teacher must create computer-based instruction appropriate for the school context and the needs of students. Predeveloped software like Feudal Lords can be used, but it is only as good as the capacity of the teacher using it to guide students' learning. This should be an obvious point, but is too often lost in the fantasy that computers can take over instruction. In fact, they require the teacher to develop curriculum very actively, in order to set the appropriate stage for their use. As Joel explains,

> Before you can do anything, there's always a baseline terminology or baseline concept that you need to deal with. We try to get that groundwork set. And then from there they have to take it and apply it somewhere. Let's say I present supply and demand. They apply that in very different ways and in different places. I give them a test on supply and on the theory and the graphs and all that stuff. Then they take those concepts to Feudal Lords, or to the marketplace. And they apply those tenets of the study to the actual game situation. There's always a direct tie from there to the concepts to the experience. Sometimes they try to beat the system embedded in the game, which is natural. I'll stop it there—if they try to bypass retailers and stuff and sell directly to the house. It's really good to develop their thinking, actually. That's the kind of stuff I would encourage.

Like the other teachers, Joel evolved his curriculum over time, by trying new ideas in the classroom, reflecting on how well they worked, then refining them continuously. He reflected on how he used his early experiences in the classroom to develop his style of teaching:

> I found out a long time ago that kids don't retain a lot of what they hear—you know, their ears are very short. They will remember it for a short period of time. But if they personalize it and take control of it and own it, whether it's Feudal Lords or an investment portfolio, it's theirs. They seem to retain it a lot better, in my experience. And so that's the reason I use that technique. I figured that out pretty early on. I would say 3 or 4 years, maybe 5 years after I started teaching. I could see what was happening—which kids in my class were successful and which weren't.

By watching the choices students made in simulations and in their interactions and from the results of the game, Joel assessed whether students were developing an understanding of the concepts taught. He did not possess a strong theoretical grounding in assessment, nor did he have the language to describe his process, but during projects he felt he had a sense of what students were learning by watching and listening to them. In addition to the project assignments, he gauged students' work through tests and research papers. He also considers the popularity of the course one indicator that students enjoy it and are learning from it.

> I can tell from the kids' feedback whether or not they're understanding what we're doing. Do they get excited about it to some degree, or is it just another assignment? That to me is the defining moment— when they personalize it and they take ownership of it as theirs. 'Cause if it's mine, it's just another lesson. If it's theirs, it becomes like an emotional experience for some of them.
>     The evidence, to me, comes when I can see whether or not they're understanding. For instance, take the marketplace game. I observe it the whole time. And they make mistakes and do things well and so forth. But I can tell whether or not they understand it just by watching them interact in the game. Could I give them a test that would do that? I don't think so.

# CHAPTER 7

# The Soul and Process of Writing: Required Sophomore English

WHEN I MET Clarence Serends, he was in his tenth year teaching at Woodland. After obtaining a degree in journalism, he worked as a sports information officer for 3 years, first in Vermont, then in Virginia. Unhappy with the lifestyle and hours required by this work, he decided to take up teaching, and so pursued a master's in education. He worked for 2 years as an English teacher in Virginia before coming to WHS.

Many of Clarence's ideas about teaching writing came from his experience as a journalist. His identity as a writer formed the basis for his teaching. Clarence began using a word processor during his sports information days; later, it became a useful tool for teaching writing. The way he used computers in his classroom was very clearly linked to his ideas on teaching writing. There were certain principles he believed were crucial to the learning process. He talked about the importance of engaging students in "play" around writing, which meant getting them to experiment with many ways of expressing themselves by varying openings, sentences, or structure. Experiments with writing, he argued, did not seem as permanent on a computer screen as they do when handwritten, which fostered more of the kind of wordplay, drafting, and redrafting he wanted to see in his classes. By doing this, he coached students in the metacognition of the writing process—learning that he hoped would stick with them.

Clarence taught several classes during the year I observed at WHS. The one I visited was called Writing Prose. Required of all 10th graders at the school, the course taught mostly nonfiction writing, which included a major research paper and other assignments that change year by year, but may include college essay writing, process description, satire, memoir, and autobiography.

The room where Clarence taught, known as the Writing Prose Room, had 23 computers around its edge—some of them older models, some newer—and a networked laser printer. Adjacent to the room was a small space with 6 additional computers, which students were allowed to use if they were not being used by another group.

During all classes I observed, each student had access to a single computer for the entire 90 minutes. Students used them as adults use their computers in an office: They worked on them when they needed to, but they were also free to work on their writing in other ways while in the classroom. When they entered the room they would turn on the computer and retrieve their work to the screen, but they also spent class time looking at hard-copy drafts, conferencing, and reading each other's work. The computers were simply available as needed.

## INSTRUCTION: THE WRITING WORKSHOP

Clarence emphasized his personal connection with students as central to drawing them into the psychology of learning to write. Each day he stood at the door greeting students as they entered the classroom. He used this interaction as a check-in: "What are you working on?" "How's it going with your college essay?" "Have you thought up a topic yet?" "Did you try what I suggested with that opening to your piece?", and most important, "What are you planning to do today?" Inside the classroom the atmosphere was like a workshop. Some students would sit right down at the computer to work on a piece of writing, perhaps popping in a CD of their favorite music and hooking up a set of earphones. Others would look through writing folders for previous drafts they needed to work on. Some students reviewed each other's work in hard copy or directly on the computer screen. The rest read drafts aloud to others, wrote new versions, or worked with Clarence's comments as they revised at the computer.

The overall structure Clarence set up was to directly teach techniques needed for different assignments (such as satire or essay), then provide a flexible, supportive atmosphere for writing and revision. Clarence would make rounds throughout the workshop-type classes, as he checked in with students. "I try to check in with each student at least once over the course of a class period," he told me. He would consult at length with quite a few students over the course of the class period, sometimes at their request, and sometimes at his.

The dynamic in the room varied from day to day, some days quite serious, others less so. Some students were able to shut out the world and do quite a bit of drafting during class; others clearly did their drafting at home, leaving revision and conferencing for school hours.

With an undergraduate degree in journalism and experience in sports information, Clarence took education courses and English courses in Virginia, then student taught. The education courses, he said, didn't supply much of a conceptual base; he found them too rigid, and the expectations for students that they conveyed exceedingly low.

> I didn't believe it. I guess I still don't believe it. . . . I just don't believe that there's that many can'ts with all the brain research and stuff that's out. So those were hard courses to sit through, because I didn't buy into it. It's the same with my students, when people tell me the kid can't do that. I always challenge it. Ok, maybe they can't, but I leave an opportunity open and see.

This absence of a theoretical base from his formal education left Clarence to develop pedagogical theories centered on what he knew about writing. His teaching philosophy combined an emphasis on positive relationships with students, high standards, and very specific ideas about how to teach writing. Clarence thought a lot about each student's individual needs, then attempted to connect with each individual positively so that when he wished to challenge them, a prior trusting relationship had already been established. This tension between trust and push is central to his philosophy.

> I'm kind of a metaphysical person. I believe that those kids were meant to be my students. So I have great joy that they are there. There's a reason that they're there. I don't know—maybe it just makes it more fun for me to believe that. But that's what I've grown to believe. And I'm very proud of their accomplishments. And when they leave I tell them they're my kids. And that when they move on, I want them to still be my kids so I still keep track of what's going on. To me, teaching is the joy of the relationship. The curriculum is second. But I'm also—I don't know if it's because my dad is a scientist or what, but—I'm also really high on if you're going to do the job, do it really, really well. So I'm known as having high standards, but I don't think they're very complex. They're very simple stuff that you just ought to be able to do very well. Like work. I mean the ability to work and to focus, and the ability to edit on your own, without having to rely on other people. And to take information that I give you, which is, for example, "you have this difficulty with commas," and take your own paper apart, looking for those particular things. To have that total determination to do it well.

He showed me an example of this process when he provided several pages of feedback on a student's writing, telling the student, "I've seen these problems all year long. You need to fix that in all your writing."

I try to get them to work for me. . . . We have a few kids who are self-driven. A lot of kids aren't. They work harder for one teacher than another because of the relationship that they have with that teacher. So I try to get that relationship in a short amount of time, because I don't have them all year. It's easier when I have had them in a previous class, because they jump in, and they know me. You support them, but they also know you mean business, and you want them—need them—to get to the next level.

Using computers to teach writing came naturally to Clarence, an extension of using them in his own writing. They became virtually indispensable to his teaching, needed to support the creativity with which he urged students to write, and the multiple drafts he required them to submit. His rationale for using computers was clearly and strongly linked to what he thinks is important in teaching writing. I asked him to imagine how it might be different if someone took away the computers and he had to teach the entire course without them. His response illustrates just how central the technology had become.

I'm not sure you could ask for as much play—you know, "Change this line." Because, without computers, you're asking them to have to rewrite the whole paper to change that line. I just don't think you would get the same level of excellence. I don't think you would get the same final product. You couldn't ask for as many revisions. With the computers, the writing excellence is higher, and I can get them to spend 3 weeks on a paper.

I think there's more ownership in a handwritten piece. I think you would fight more students on changing things. Once they get it down on paper, it's very difficult to get it off. On a computer screen they are a little more flexible about changing things.

Playing is important. I can't overemphasize that. Stopping and saying, "I don't like that word. How can I rephrase that? How can I do this?" Moving things around. That's the whole beauty of it. "I didn't like that beginning. Let met try this." Or, "I liked the beginning I had before. Well, it's all still there. I didn't cut it out. I'm just playing with it."

In the beginning I think I did the old first draft, second draft, final, and you're done. And now for some students I require eight drafts, because there's more to work on. With another student, the level of play might be to a point where I ask him or her do it one more time, until I say "Let's move on to the next paper for you, because you've gotten as much as you can out of this one." With the computers, I can have them do drafts until I feel like we've milked as much learning experience from that draft as we're going to get, or I sense frustration over the topic.

That's the advantage of the computer. Writing doesn't have to be beginning-to-end like it was when we were typing it. So if it's right in your mind—"Wow, I'd really like that"—just type it in. No one has ever told them to do that: Just type it in. And worry about the beginning later, and do the cut and paste and go crazy with it, trying what comes to mind.

Clarence has constructed his way of teaching writing, providing multiple assignments with frequent revisions, with the capabilities of the word processor in mind and at hand. He laid out the goals for the course as follows:

I want kids to have heard about how to develop the structure of an essay or the point of an essay from the audience's point of view. To design and to play around with the language that they are using, as well as the word choice, to get a piece that is interesting, informative, and well-structured. I also believe there is a secondary goal: that they can use a computer as simply as their pencil so that they're erasing and experimenting, so it becomes a very natural tool for them.

In each assignment he stressed work on a different element of writing: brainstorming, strong beginnings, organization. He always emphasized improvements in grammar, spelling, and punctuation, and developed a handout called The Naughty Nine, which addressed mistakes his students commonly make.

Students had to be willing to attempt multiple drafts and extensive revisions. This was not always easy to teach. One technique he used occasionally with some students was to hide their work on the server so it was difficult to find. This created a situation where the student had to begin writing again. Clarence used this to show the student that starting over again can sometimes yield better writing than just editing what you've got. He pointed out that he only does this as students are beginning a paper, and only with those whom he thinks will be able to handle it. It encouraged them to rethink their original approach, he maintained, and to learn that a completely new draft can be more powerful and nuanced than the first.

"Gosh it's gone." "How about trying it my way this time—just try it." I can't use it on a person who is a computer nut, because she'll find the file. Because I don't hide it very far. I change the name of it so that they can't find it through the name, and I put it somewhere, but a person could figure it out if they had plenty of time. Sometimes I tell them that I did that on purpose, and sometimes I don't. I'll probably pick a student I have a decent relationship with too. They'll trust me and then go along with the process.

Clarence developed other techniques through his own knowledge of the writing process rather than having seen them anywhere. He would ask a student who was experiencing writing block to turn off her screen and type for 15 to 20 minutes without looking. This would encourage the student to write freely without worrying about every word. When she would turn the monitor back on, she would have already begun her piece, having worked her way through the block. Clarence would occasionally direct students to work for a while on an assignment, then switch computers, in order to read their neighbor's work and comment on it. This encouraged peer editing.

Since each student worked at his or her own pace, Clarence had to develop a system for checking with them at the beginning of each class period and insisting that they make progress that day:

I hold them at the door to the room, before they enter each day. "I want to know what your topic is or which piece you're working on." If that was their homework for the weekend, and if they don't have it, they sit in the hall until they give me something. So I'm more protective of the room at the beginning of the process. I make it a privilege to be in the room. They're there to work, to write. They're not there to think about something that should have been done over the weekend. It's hard to enforce that when you're working one-on-one in writing conferences—it's hard to walk around and make sure people are working. So you kind of fire things out while you're doing the writing conference. But ideally I'm walking around and checking on what people are doing, and if the person who hasn't spent time [at home working on the writing], I take him or her out, I take them to another classroom or something, and say, "I want you to grab a seat." Or I bring them to the student who's helping me teach, or I pair them off with someone who I know is really creative, and say to that person, "Can you spend 10 minutes with so-and-so, and help her brainstorm some topics?"

More recently, Clarence has begun using computers for classroom research:

I like it because when you do research on the computers your kids are in the classroom. It still happens sometimes where kids have to go to the library, but the periodical database we have is on some computers right in the classroom. You can see their research skills right in front of you. When you allow them to leave the classroom, who knows what they're doing in the library? I can group kids together in the room next door, saying, "That's going to be the research room today, and you can keep the word processing going in this other room." I don't have to lose them to the library. So you kind of have a thumb on what's going on, perhaps a bit more.

## PROFESSIONAL LEARNING: DEVELOPING A PEDAGOGY BASED ON THE WRITING PROCESS

Clarence began using computers during his work in public relations. When he worked in Virginia in sports information, around 1985, he began using spreadsheets to keep statistics, and word processing for writing and publishing. During his student teaching, he had some additional exposure to the possibilities of working with computers. Although in the beginning this experience was fraught with technical difficulties, it gave Clarence a sense of what the possibilities were and fueled his commitment to use computers in the classroom.

> During my student teaching it was cool; IBM did something with the University of Virginia, where they gave all the student teachers a laptop with a little tiny printer clipped on the back. It was like a little tape paper like you see on an adding machine. And my master teacher, the professor who was teaching the course, and the classes they were teaching would all log on at the same time. And so we would have a discussion at home. It rarely worked, but when it did, it was quite cool. And then we had to hand the machine back. The quality of the printing was horrible, so we didn't use it like they wanted us to use it. They wanted us to do all our stuff on it. But it was easier to use a computer that you had for yourself. We went through the e-mail system at UVA. It was really great. It wasn't as powerful as having the person there and talking, but it was a nice idea, and it linked us all together. It was called Teacher-Link.

I asked how he learned to use computers for teaching writing the way he does. Consistent with the general pattern followed by other teachers in this study, Clarence had a set of experiences from which he built technical knowledge. At the same time, he matched this knowledge to his theory of learning, gradually building a curriculum.

Just trial and error. No one taught me. There was a summer institute here on teaching writing. It was 1989 maybe, and they invited me to speak for 25 minutes on it, because I had done the Writing Prose course, and I guess I was being looked at as someone who used technology a lot, which is just word processing.

People were asking me about how I do it, and I said, "I have no idea, really." I think you have some sort of assignment that kids can play with, that's not fill in the blanks and stuff and just let them go, and then be over their shoulder a lot. Don't ever sit at a desk and watch. Just walk around, sit down with them, do a ton of mini-conferencing, and see what happens.

Clarence knows a lot about writing and teaching writing, but did not always have the language to describe how he taught or how he learned to teach, reflecting the limited theory he said he obtained in his formal education training. In the several years prior to the research, he participated in workshops on using the Internet for research. He specifically mentioned workshops sponsored by the district, in which they learned to use ProQuest, a database of periodicals. After that, when his students worked on their major research paper for the term, one of their options would be to conduct their research right in the classroom.

Like the other teachers, Clarence's way of working in the classroom evolved over the course of years. When he first arrived at WHS, he was a substitute teacher, taught without computers, and was following a curriculum not his own. He credits an administrator who worked with him, but who is no longer at the school, for encouraging him to discover his own way of working with students rather than forcing him into a rigid model.

When I spoke with him about his professional learning, Clarence's reflections revolved around how to strengthen his writing instruction, and how to connect with students better, so that he could challenge them more:

> The part I'd like to improve on is connecting reading and writing. I've never been trained in it. And I would like to know more about it, because a college professor told me that I wasn't doing it correctly, that I need to have a lot more reading in my courses in order to make the writing improve. I do believe that, but I need to have more time to work on that with someone who has done it. I believe you show students, for example, a satire. What's a good satire. You discuss the elements of a good satire. You show them what it looks like, ideally. If you have previous student work that's read aloud, that's the standard you shoot for.

He adjusts his curriculum and teaching year to year depending on the feedback he has received from students about what they learned and on the quality of their writing at the end of the course. At the beginning of the semester, he would conduct a preassessment, in which the students write one draft of an assignment. He would save this to compare to their work at the end of the semester, which consists of a final exam and a reflective letter on what they have learned.

> Their final assignment is to write me a grammatically perfect—as well as they can—letter about their experience in my class. That's one of the parts of the exam. I list all the assignments they have done, and ask, "Which assignment worked for you? Which didn't? Do you think your writing improved? What kind of additional help could you have gotten? Is this a different experience than what you had before?"
>
> I change every year based on the data I collect. For example, I no longer give certain papers—a definition paper, and another paper— because students hated them. So I don't do it.

The feedback he has received from students has also changed his way of working in the classroom, because he perceived that the needs of some were not being met.

> Most of the students want more access to me. They tell me, "I wish we could have worked on this more. When you said that I didn't understand it." I have to be real careful, because certain kids pull me every single day. And I have to be able to say to some of those, "Last time in class I helped you," and move on to someone else. I've gotten better at keeping track of where the kids are and that's probably from the feedback I've gotten. A student might say something in the final letter I would have had no clue about. "I had trouble with that paper." Well, I never knew that.

He also defined his success and failure based on his relationship with students, his ability to push them past the limits they set for themselves:

> I connect my own success or failure to whether the kids have made a connection with me. If there are two or three kids in that class who still haven't made a connection with me, I look back, and say, "That wasn't an effective teaching job." Because there wasn't any inspiration there. I didn't make a personal contact, so the writing is pretty normal.

At WHS, Clarence is one of the teachers known for his use of classroom technology. Computers are not critical to his core philosophy of establishing a trusting relationship with students, yet they are critical to his theory that in order to write, one must feel free to experiment, discard, revise, and revise again. Computers, then, help Clarence solve a pedagogical issue he sees as central to teaching writing. His commitment to using computers comes as an outgrowth of his own work in a previous career. Because of this previous exposure, Clarence came to see computers as a natural part of the writing process, and has extended that to his teaching.

# Powering Up Business Tools:
# A Course in Entrepreneurship

BRIGHT, ENERGETIC, and well-organized, Clarissa was the sole business teacher at WHS at the time of this study. Clarissa saw herself as building and defending the existing business education program at the school. She knew that at Woodland, because of the value placed on computer use, building a strong technology component in the program would help ensure that the business department would grow and thrive. That drive, the important role of technology in business, and the fact that she had always used computers in her professional life, meant that they were simply a natural extension of her work at all levels. As the youngest teacher in this study, Clarissa is a good example of what we may expect as teachers come through college and teacher education programs using computers all along the way.

The year I visited was Clarissa's sixth year of teaching, five of them at Woodland. Prior to teaching, she worked as an administrator at the state university, and during college interned with a large computer company nearby. She has an associate's degree in business, and a bachelor's in business education. Before coming to WHS, she worked at a different Vermont high school for a year, also teaching business subjects and utilizing computers. At that school, she taught mostly from a vocational education perspective, and also ran courses for adults to teach them software.

Clarissa was easily able to learn new software, then incorporate it into her teaching. She began using computers while in college during the 1980s, beginning with WordStar. As WordStar became outdated in the 1990s, Clarissa taught herself new word processing programs and the spreadsheet Lotus 1-2-3. The business program she attended at a local college required "a lot of technology pieces," including databases, spreadsheets, and word processing. She also took a management systems class, where she learned to use spreadsheet-type applications for information processing in business; and during her corporate internship, she observed how computer applications were used in a business setting. When she went on to study teaching, her business education curriculum always included computer use. She assumes that computers will be part of any school business program.

In her first teaching job, she found that the specific hardware and software available were different from what she already knew, so she had to teach herself Microsoft Works. Still, from her first year of teaching, she found a way to use software tools to teach marketing. When Clarissa arrived at WHS the following year, she began using Macintoshes. Once again she had to take her existing skills and retool them for new hardware and software.

## INSTRUCTION: INTEGRATING COMPUTERS
## INTO THE BUSINESS WORLD

Clarissa taught several business courses as well as computer applications. She recommended I observe her Entrepreneurship course because it would provide a case of integrating computers with the teaching of a subject, and because she was planning to develop some new uses for computers in that course. The classroom where Clarissa taught, on the building's second floor, had 18 computers around its perimeter and movable work tables in the center. The computers were available for students during in-class work time. As with all the classes I observed at WHS, when the computers were not needed, they did not pose a distraction, and students chose to use them in a wide variety of ways to suit the needs of their work on any particular day.

Clarissa's approach to the Entrepreneurship course was project based. She centered her courses on a main project or series of projects designed to highlight key concepts and allow students to develop new skills. She created a classroom with a strong structure rooted in projects and assignments, but which also allowed for considerable flexibility in how students approached the work and how they used their time. Clarissa alternated between working with the whole class of students to present key issues and concepts, and allowing students in-class time to work on assignments, which were a mixture of individual and group assignments. She presented a syllabus at the beginning of the course, including an overview of all topics and major projects, which let the students know where they were in the curriculum and where they were going. She referred to the schedule often, in a way that made the students active participants in the flow and schedule of the work.

That year Clarissa was planning to use computers for the Entrepreneurship course more intensively than she had in the past. The previous spring she had received a grant of software and support from Microsoft. As a result, she would work this year to have students create a Web site for the course and integrate Visual Basic (an object-oriented programming language) into their work, in addition to their usual use of word processing, spreadsheets, databases, and the Web for research.

The cornerstone project of the course was to produce a business plan. Each student was required to develop a concept for a small business, then plan for getting it started, including strategies for finance, marketing, and hiring personnel. Throughout, computers were integral to the course, used for word processing, graphics development, and calculations. When not working on their business plans or engaged in whole-class activities such as lecture or discussion, students were assigned to several groups, one of which developed a Web site for the course, and another that attempted to create an application of Visual Basic for business. The climate that prevailed in the class combined structure, flexibility, and Clarissa's cheerful sense of humor and upbeat personality.

Clarissa's pedagogical approach was characterized by embedding focused lessons within larger projects, in the belief that she should build a set of concepts, then allow students to try them out on their own.

> I think my philosophy has really evolved as I became more comfortable teaching. At first I thought in order to be a good teacher, you really had to be in control of everything that's going on. And that means you're in the front of the room, spouting off your knowledge. And the students are like frantically taking notes, because you know it all. By the time I got to WHS, having become more comfortable, and after working in a vocational center too, I think it changed my perspective of what my role is. Now I think that it's much more important to be there as a resource or a facilitator, and provide some structure.
>
> But it's really important, too, for the kids to be out there and experimenting hands-on. What I find the most challenging with that, though, is finding that fine line between giving enough structure so that the students know what the expectations are without giving so much structure that you're stifling the creative part. That's the challenge for me. I think that's why I might have trouble in my younger classes, like with freshman and sophomores, who maybe need more structure. I think you have to find that fine line, but the important piece is being a facilitator and letting kids research on their own.

She believed that her strategy of requiring students to dig in on realistic projects meant they could become the problem solvers they would need to be in the business world.

> I think part of it is just my belief that if I'm truly preparing them for what they are going to be facing when they leave me, then they have to be able to work as independent people. They have to be able to

problem-solve on their own, because they're not going to have a strong support like they do in school. They will need to be able to say, "I don't know how to solve this. What do I do? Where can I go to find the answer? I'm going to look in the manual"; or "I experienced this before in this work, maybe I can try this solution." To me that's really important. I mean that's the most important thing I think that you can teach them. Because the content they can learn on their own.

Clarissa's philosophy about using computers was that they simply had to be part of business education. She was the only teacher in this group who told me that computers *must* be part of the curriculum; that helping students learn to use the applications was part of what she must teach. The other teachers had a more instrumental view of the computers: they were only as valuable as they were useful for teaching subject matter. But for Clarissa, they were part of that subject matter.

To me, I'm a technology teacher, even if I use more application software than directly working with design or that sort of thing. I think that a lot of business teachers—at least from what I know of my organization, the Vermont Business Teachers Association—a lot of the business teachers are double-certified in computer science. So that that's a background I think that's absolutely crucial.

I think that for content area teachers to be teaching without technology is a real disservice to kids. I think technology motivates and excites kids. Getting on the Internet and doing research is great for most kids, although doing Internet research is sometimes stressful for kids too. Because you don't get a quick answer. But it's more fun and exciting than always going to the library. I think using technology teaches kids to express themselves in different ways. I see it working really effectively with students who might struggle a little more with school.

## PROFESSIONAL LEARNING: A COMPUTER USER FROM THE BEGINNING

The conceptual basis for Clarissa's integration of technology began during the mid-1980s, through her own experience studying business and her internship in the computer industry. For her, computers are a natural part of the business world and thus a natural part of business education. Starting from this idea, and with early exposure to basic software applications such as word processing and database management, she continued to learn new, updated software as necessary. She always sought to incorporate computer use into her courses, whether she was teaching adults or adolescents.

Mostly, she taught herself new software from manuals and experimentation. As far as classroom practice, she was also influenced by the Vermont Association of Business Teachers, which develops curriculum and circulates ideas. Clarissa attended conferences, had contacts outside the school, and spent time on the association's Web site and e-mail lists to get ideas.

As a young teacher focused on business education, Clarissa's grounding in technology occurred during college and was extended during her teacher education. Over the years, she had opportunities to use her ease with computers to develop programs teaching a range of courses. The only teacher of the five to have had significant experience with computers during college, Clarissa provides a sense of what a new generation of teachers might look like.

For her Entrepreneurship class, Clarissa applied for and received a grant of software and support to integrate Microsoft Office into the curriculum. So although the course itself was not new, some of the technological approaches were. Her specific technology-related plans were to have students build a Web site and create a business application using Visual Basic.

During the semester when I observed her teaching, Clarissa attempted these two new uses. Within the course, she created groups of students who pursued different projects throughout the semester. I made it a point to observe the Web site group and the Visual Basic group most closely, focusing on students' work, on Clarissa's interactions with them, and her reflections on how things were going. This provided an opportunity for me to observe her learning as she tested a new use of technology in the classroom.

The purpose of the Web site group was, as Clarissa put it, "to learn to use the Internet as a business tool and develop Web sites for their own businesses." The Web site group was the easier of the two for her to manage. One student in the group was quite familiar with the process of creating a Web site, and led the group in developing content. Other students in the group also seemed quite familiar with computers. The students had two different types of software from which to choose, and each of these had a "wizard" that helped them build the site. Clarissa checked on their progress from time to time, assisted them in accessing the two software packages, showed them how to use the wizard in each, and set up an appropriate account on the school's server. She was available to coach them as they set up pages, suggesting commands to try or directing them to online help or hard-copy manuals. It all went fairly smoothly.

The Visual Basic group posed a greater challenge. Three students volunteered for this group. All three seemed quite comfortable using computers, and one had done a bit of BASIC programming previously. As part of the grant she obtained, Clarissa was supposed to receive extensive documentation, teaching manuals, and support for the new software. Her own copy of Visual Basic did not arrive during the previous summer as expected, but rather in the fall, leaving her limited time during the busy school year to learn the software herself before trying it in the classroom. Little supporting documentation ever arrived, though some was available within the software itself.

Students in this group were assigned to "develop an application useful for business." First, they would have to familiarize themselves with what the software could do, develop an idea for an application, and finally create it. Due to her unfamiliarity, Clarissa was at a loss to show them specifics, but directed them to the tutorial in the application, offering them the opportunity to take it home. The students did not sit and find their way through the tutorial, preferring mostly to rely on a student who used some prior knowledge of programming to program a few objects. Apparently, however, they did complete some of this work at home. In the end, the group created an application that processed payroll and deductions. It was a triumph that they were able to create such a program, though the experience was not what their teacher had originally hoped it would be.

I asked Clarissa to talk about this experience. She reflected on her usual way of learning a piece of software, and found the process less workable for Visual Basic:

> The one I've been the most challenged by is the Visual Basic, and I didn't get it for the summer. And I didn't get any resources with that, like I did for Microsoft Office. For the most part I can teach myself applications from the manual. But with Visual Basic, I haven't been able to do that as well. I've had to sit down myself and go through the tutorials, but I don't apply the tutorials immediately. So that's been the only software I've been unable to find my way through by using what I already know about other software.

However, she had already reflected on what had occurred in the classroom and made plans for improving it next year:

> One of my goals for next summer is to really sit down and come up with my own kind of manual for students on how they can develop a simple Visual Basic program. I want to do that rather than just saying, like I did this year, "OK, you sit down, and you go through the tutorial, and take advantage of these little hodgepodge minutes that I give you and try to come up with a cohesive project." I don't think that's going to happen. How I imagined it working was that I would have had more time to go through the tutorial myself. And

that I would have been a better asset to the students. I'm not this year. I can't answer their questions. And that frustrates me. I like that comfort level of at least being able to look through the different menus and kind of know what I'm looking for, and by trial and error find what it is we need to do. And I don't feel comfortable doing that with the Visual Basic yet. So my goal is to learn that software and get a better comfort level with it, or at least be able to problem-solve better, and come up with something that students can use, rather than relying on the tutorial.

She reflected as well on how she might have worked differently with the group, and what she would do with them next time.

Front-loading them with some ideas beforehand would have been helpful, because yesterday was the first day I heard them kind of excited like, "Wow! We can do this payroll thing." We had just finished doing the payroll piece, and that must have prompted them. I told the students, "You could use it to keep track of your customer information, or you could use it for inventory, to be the program where you plug all your inventory in." I don't think it really clicked for them how efficient that software could make a business until they did the payroll piece.

They had been saying how tedious it was to keep records of everything and remember all the percentage deductions, so that you know how much tax you have to send in, things like that. So I think if I can give them some examples and show them some beforehand, then I can say, "OK. You can see how that works, now we can do it for your business." But I do want the idea to be developed by them, rather than me saying, "I want you to create such and such." So they had the freedom to do that. Then they take ownership over it; they're not doing it for me; they're doing it to learn the technology.

Clarissa also talked about how the time it takes to use technology makes it a challenge to cover the entire curriculum, and how she thought about making her students' computer use mesh more tightly with hers. She put considerable thought into this issue and her teaching, such that we were always talking about improvements, whether during our informal conversations or informal interviews. At one point I asked her what, based on her experience this year, she planned to do differently with next year's course.

Entrepreneurship is really the class I'm most passionate about, and so I think my mind is always a mush of how I can do things better and do things differently. At one point I thought about doing basic entrepreneurship for kids who might want to do that, and have the second part of Entrepreneurship be about integrating technology into a business setting. There we would cover what kinds of things you would use—and have that be an elective piece of the course.

There is this constant frustration of how we can get beyond word processing into entrepreneurship. And where will I find the time to do that? I feel like I don't have enough time to sacrifice something else, because every day that we're there we build on our business plan. I can't sacrifice a piece of their business plan to spend a day talking about how you use Publisher. So one of the things I'm thinking about is making it much more directive, telling them, "These are the steps you go through. You can do your business card, for example, on Publisher," then have them do it. I just keep thinking that by the time they are seniors they should have a lot more computer and technology experience than they do. But I can't make knowing that technology a prerequisite or I wouldn't have the students I have. It's almost like I need to have a workshop in technology before they come to Entrepreneurship. That would be what I would really like.

Clarissa felt that breaking the course into two pieces: a first semester where it was just the business plan, and a second semester that focused on using technology in business, might resolve some of the time-related tension she felt when teaching students to use software. A theme for Clarissa was how to manage to integrate every application she thought important and still have time to cover the business concepts. She was trying to reorder her curriculum to accommodate all this. For her, development and refinement of her curriculum was a major focus that year.

Writing about the lives of teachers, Michael Huberman (1989, 1993) describes a typical career trajectory. Following an initial phase he calls "survival and discovery," and a subsequent period of "stabilization" in which the individual commits to teaching, Huberman identifies a stage of "experimentation/activism." This is when "the gradual consolidation of an instructional repertoire leads naturally to attempts to increase one's impact," and is characterized by experimentation with materials, pupil groupings, curriculum sequencing, and so forth. At the same time, the desire to increase one's impact leads to awareness of institutional problems and the desire to change them (1989, p. 34).

The experimentation/activism phase characterized Clarissa's approach to her work at the time of this study. She was deeply involved with refining her curriculum and experimenting with new techniques—especially ones that were technology based. She was consciously working to retain and expand the business program at the school. Since she saw computers as integral both to business education and to the mission of the school, building the business program by increasing its use of technology was appropriate and appealing to her. Clarissa was a young, active teacher who was consolidating her teaching skills while simultaneously becoming aware of her organizational role in the school. This stance cemented her commitment to the school's technology committee, and her sense of herself as a person who could have an impact at the school. Such an attitude was welcomed by her colleagues and the school's administration.

# Teacher Learning and Organizational Culture: Implications for Leadership and Policy

IN PART III, we move from the stories of teachers as individuals to examine the commonalities in their learning and explore how those processes were supported by the school and district organizations. This necessitates considering structural elements such as resources, time, incentives, and organization, but it also involves analysis of how the norms and ideas that pervaded the school's culture shape the environment for professional learning. These values, norms, and ideas make up the cultural constructs that guide teachers' understanding of their work, their ongoing choices about what is important, and what will be accepted or admired by others in their social setting. In this final section, I describe the processes common to the five teachers' learning, then set them within the cultural context of the school.

# CHAPTER 9

# Teacher Learning: How New Uses of Technology Are Created in Classrooms

THE FIVE TEACHERS I studied at Woodland differed in their developmental paths, the subjects they taught, the resources they used, and their actual instructional practice, yet their learning had the five common elements mentioned in Chapter 3:

- Making a commitment to use computers
- Defining instructional problems
- Scanning for new ideas and practices
- Creating new curriculum and practice
- Trying, reflecting, and refining in the classroom

Here, I explore each of these in further detail, drawing additional examples from the now familiar case studies to illustrate how the teachers' learning occurred.

## THE COMMITMENT TO USE COMPUTERS

Learning to use hardware and software, overcoming technological glitches, adjusting the culture of the classroom to fit computer use, creating lessons, and persevering when lessons don't work out as planned make the process of integration a very challenging one. As the five teachers told their stories, it became clear that their learning, while supported by the organization and driven to some extent by school expectations, required the focus and perspicacity to push beyond the usual expectations of a teacher. Learning to use computers in the classroom, which means creating new practice with technology that supports a teacher's pedagogical goals and students' needs, simply requires so much work that only a teacher who already sees its value will carry it out. As the stories of these five teachers illustrate, it is not that full commitment must come before any learning at all, but rather that the teacher had to be sold on the idea that computers could be instructionally worthwhile before he or she would dig into the hard work of integrating them with instruction.

Everett Rogers (1995) studied how and why people adopt innovations, and out of this coined the law of relative advantage. He argued that people adopt innovations depending on "the degree to which an innovation is perceived as being better than the idea it supersedes" (p. 12). The teachers at Woodland who used technology in their teaching felt that using technology would, in some circumstances, be better than not using it. This meant that they were willing to spend time learning about hardware and software, managing and caring for the machines, and developing lessons and curriculum that utilized computers. Therefore, if school leaders are looking for high-quality, thorough, and deep integration of technology into the curriculum, they need to think about what will convince their teachers that it's worth doing at all.

Each of these five teachers began using computers back in the early 1980s, and can describe how their thinking about technology and their classroom work with it developed over the intervening years. Their learning process evolved slowly, requiring years of focus: in time, energy, the effort to learn and relearn, discipline, and the willingness to take risks in the classroom. These teachers' sense of commitment increased over the years as they learned more about using technology and as the technology itself became more advanced and more accessible. For them, using computers made sense given what they sought to accomplish in the classroom.

## Ambivalents and Nonusers

For contrast, I interviewed teachers who used computers less intensively in the classroom (whom I call *ambivalents*) or not at all (*nonusers*). Just as the commitment of the teachers in the case studies depended on their perceptions of technology's usefulness, so the ambivalents and nonusers registered considerably less conviction that using computers was worthwhile.

I asked one of the ambivalent teachers in the English department, Elsa, why she didn't use computers more frequently in her classroom, especially since they were such a prominent feature of the school. At first, she said it was because she had limited access to computers for her students. But when I explored that statement further with her, she began to say that using computers didn't match her instructional mode, particularly for her classes that focused on literary analysis:

I don't want to use up class time having students sit at a computer typing when they can do that at home. Now that most students have computers at home, and there are enough computers in the school, they all have access to computers. They do all that work at home. They bring in their paper. I edit it. I give it back to them. They go off. So I feel that time should be better spent. And I'm not into having them get on the Internet and have pen pals in other countries. Some of the teachers do that. They have Web pages where they publish their stuff. I don't know the technology myself that well. I still teach English the old-fashioned way most of the time.

Here she is saying two things: that she doesn't know how to use the computers that well and she's not sure if she wants to. I asked her if she would use the computers more often if she did have access to them:

I wouldn't want access to the computers all the time. It doesn't matter to me. Because, well, I suppose if I had, I mean, my ideal situation would be a big room with maybe a row of five computers in the back, and students could have access to those during part of the period, maybe to work together. It would be nice to have Internet access right there in the room, when we're trying to look up some-thing right away. But I wouldn't necessarily want to have a computer for every student in English 10. I still think there's a lot of value to students sitting in a circle, discussing a book. I mean, no way is a computer going to be able to replicate that.

Her argument that she would not use them was based on her theories about teaching English literature and writing—that they would not help her that much. Elsa was somewhat interested in more access to computers for research and mentioned that she would like to explore additional possibili-ties for their use, but was clearly ambivalent about the value of the machines for helping her teach literature. This ambivalence meant that she did not struggle for increased access and that her commitment to learning more about using the technology for teaching was limited.

Ron, a social studies teacher who uses computers personally and main-tains his own, quite interesting, Web site, was most explicit about his hesita-tion to dive into teaching with the machines. Although Ron could see the value of the Internet for students conducting research, he worried about its limitations when compared to book research. When I inquired why he didn't use computers more in the classroom, especially since he seemed so com-fortable with them, he succinctly captured what I had heard from other am-bivalent teachers when he said: "The balance just hasn't tipped for me yet

with this stuff." He was not "resisting change," as some might characterize his hesitation. Rather, he was using his judgment as a teacher to decide
which tools were best for his students. He did use the Internet for some
research, but like Elsa, he was not convinced that the pedagogical value of
using the machines sufficiently improved the quality of what he could do
in the classroom.

Elsa and Ron did not fear new technology, nor were they averse to
change. They outlined rational, pedagogically based reasons for not being
more committed to computer use. Both teachers connected instructional
choices to their level of interest in using computers.

Another teacher with whom I spoke chose to use a different technology, but not computers, because that technology aligned best with his pedagogical thinking. A veteran math teacher, he used graphing calculators with
his students because he wanted each student to have one, and they are cheaper
and smaller than computers. Among other things, he used the calculators in
class by showing students how entering different values for variables in an
equation produces graphs of different shape or slope.

Two other teachers at the school, both long-term veterans, were no-
torious nonusers of computers. Although virtually all faculty at WHS used
e-mail for routine communication, these two were well known for their re-
luctance to do so; they certainly would not consider using computers for
teaching. The first, an art teacher, simply didn't like the medium provided
by computers: "I don't like the idea of the screen or the smallness. . . . I
like the differences in all kinds of media that we work with in art and hate
to see it limited to a screen." She was not enthusiastic about the prospects
of technology for her, and simply didn't want to bother with it. The second, a well-respected English teacher who retired at the end of the year,
felt that teaching writing with computers fostered bad habits in the students. She felt that tearing up a first draft and beginning anew was an essential part of writing. Students who use word processors, she argued, just
cut and paste, never attempting a fresh start; they piece their writing together
and never learn to work start to finish. She refused to use computers to teach
writing because she felt it could damage students' long-term progress as they
learned.

At WHS, teachers' choices about whether to commit to learning about
computers and use them for instruction were strongly rooted in pedagogical
reasoning. Of course, it is not really so simple: Concerns about access, classroom management, and the time necessary to develop new teaching practice
also emerged. In the case of the Foreign Language Department, teachers had
access to computers for several years in the form of a lab used mostly for teaching about the culture of Spanish-speaking countries. Several teachers used the
lab, but some glitches in networked software, as well as disagreement about

what kind of support was needed, led eventually to its underuse and dismantling. Several foreign language teachers told me that they definitely would use computers if they were easily available, but since access was a problem, they had stopped. However, these same teachers generally were not sure how they would use them if they did gain access, and usually expressed ambivalence—again on pedagogical grounds—at some point during the interview. Teachers who claimed they had too little access were also less convinced of the instructional value of the computers and less willing to work the internal political system of the school to gain increased access.

Did teachers not use the computers because they didn't have access to them? Or did they decline to push for access because they weren't interested in using the computers? At this school, I think the latter explanation prevails. Teachers who really wanted the computers for their classroom worked the political system to ensure their access, either through being active on the technology committee or talking directly to the principal. In fact, it wasn't very difficult to get access to computers at WHS. An application from a teacher usually set the gears in motion, even though it might take a few years to ramp up to full availability.

Some studies on innovation in schools have argued that teachers may only commit to a new practice after they attempt it. Huberman and Miles (1984) argue that in a group of schools they studied, institutionalization of instructional innovations was accomplished through "mandated, stable use," where schools and central offices required an innovation and put pressure on teachers to try it. They argue that in this group, "user mastery and commitment" followed, leading to "stabilized use" (pp. 17–18).

In these schools, belief in the value of the innovation usually followed attempts made by teachers who were mandated to use the innovation. However, in a second group of schools in the same study, outcomes almost as high were accomplished through a strategy of "skillful, committed use," in which schools "did not mandate the innovation, but spent much energy on assisting users and developing their commitment" (p. 18). The second group of schools studied by Huberman and Miles was more similar to WHS: Urging and support from school and district leadership, through a variety of strategies, served to develop commitment and individual learning.

In a world without resource constraints, I suppose that computers could be made widely available so that teachers could explore using them when and how they see fit. However, that is not reality, and it would be wasteful to equip and update classrooms where computers are not used. The teachers' decision to adopt classroom technology should therefore be considered an early part of their learning. Essentially, they have to decide *whether* the computers are worth using before they can learn *how* to use them in the classroom; otherwise, they do not focus sufficiently on the learning process to work through all the barriers they encounter. The commitment–learning cycle can be slow and intertwined with other factors, but only those who were convinced of the technology's pedagogical value really dug in and integrated them with instruction.

In cases where teachers did use computers extensively, they perceived this relative advantage: that they were better off with them than without them, that the computers helped solve educational problems about which teachers were concerned. They perceived this advantage from the outset, and it was this that allowed them to commit. On the other hand, where teachers were more hesitant about using the computers, they were unsure that the work involved would be worth all the trouble. Their commitment wavered, and so they did not as aggressively pursue technology-related professional learning.

## DEFINING INSTRUCTIONAL PROBLEMS

The teachers in these cases employed technology to assist with challenges in their teaching. Motivating students to write and revise; helping them make connections between history and literature; promoting scientific thinking in the form of hypothesis formulation and testing; simulating the real world: All were instructional goals teachers facilitated with computer technology. The teachers found technology that would enhance their work with students in ways they saw as important—even critical—to their work. If they were convinced that computers in general might be valuable, they used them to help solve particular challenges they experienced in their teaching.

Each of the five teachers adopted a computer application that fit within his or her general theory of pedagogy to solve a previously identified instructional problem. These teachers had strong pedagogical theories, explicit or tacit theories about how students learn and how they should teach. Like all professionals, they struggled to solve problems and issues in their practice. Their interest in classroom technology allowed them to expand their general theories to include technology and consider it as a possible solution.

The connection between teachers' beliefs about learning and their pedagogical decisions was stated well by Olson and Bruner in 1996:

> Our interactions with others are deeply affected by our everyday intuitive theories about how our own minds and minds of others work. These theories, rarely made explicit, are omnipresent in practical and educational decisions. . . . Teaching then, is inevitably based on teachers' notions about the nature of the learner's mind. Beliefs and assumptions about teaching, whether in a school or in any other context, are a direct reflection of the beliefs and assumptions the teacher holds about the learner. (p. 9).

Some of the teachers were able to articulate their theories to me. For others, their theories became obvious through observing their work and asking them about it. Writing about the relationship between teachers' thinking and their work, Pope (1993) argues:

> Much of teacher craft thinking is tacit—i.e. know-how gained through experience and not usually articulated. Autobiographies may reveal something of this tacit knowledge provided that these are also related to current everyday classroom problems that teachers experience. (p. 25)

The teachers' theories guided the decisions they made about curriculum and instruction, including what was problematic in the classroom and whether using technology might help address the problems. The cognitive perspective on this holds that we can understand the teacher as "a constructivist who continually builds, elaborates, and tests his or her personal theory of the world" (Clark, 1986, p. 9). The theories teachers hold about learning guide their decisions in minute-by-minute classroom interactions, day-by-day decisions on lesson planning, and with regard to larger scale decisions about which innovations are worth adopting and which ones to leave aside.

These pedagogical theories constitute the cognitive framework a teacher uses to make countless decisions over the course of a class period, a day, a semester, a year, and a career. They guide decisions about everything over which the teacher has control: setting up a classroom's physical space, rules of conduct, curriculum, texts and resources, assignments, groupings, how to ask a question, how to answer a question, what grades to give, how to respond to homework, how hard to push a student, how structured to be, or how loose. The teachers in this study weighed decisions they made in the classroom against the general question: "How will this affect my students' learning?" Exactly how they formulate this question and how they answer it was guided by their pedagogical philosophy.

The five teachers discussed here derived their working theories from a very wide range of sources. They were influenced by their own experiences at school or college, by professional programs, student teaching, professional networks and publications in their subject area, day-to-day classroom experience, their colleagues and friends, and the prevailing culture of the school. Based on their personal theories, each teacher had a sense of working on an aspect of his or her practice. One might be working on better connections with students, another on stimulating interest in intellectually rigorous topics, and a third on helping students stick with the challenges of analyzing scientific data. When they encountered students not learning as well as they liked, they thought about why and developed a hypothesis. They sought to help students understand relationships between physical variables, develop their voices as writers, or go beyond abstract descriptions of economic systems. They looked around for solutions to these problems, problems which they had defined themselves. So, as these teachers developed their work with technology, it was linked to a problem of practice with which they were fully engaged. While technology may not have been the only answer, it was an important possible solution to the daily challenges they faced within their curriculum, alongside their students.

This kind of problem definition is a hallmark of professional-level work. The teachers' use of technology connected well to their overall philosophies about how children learn and how they should teach their particular subject matter. The two became intertwined: When asked about their philosophies on how to use technology, the teachers wove pedagogical theories into their responses. And when asked about their philosophy of teaching, use of technology was often a prominent feature in the answer.

The literature on adult learning in the workplace highlights the act of defining problems as an important characteristic of professional activity. In work where people encounter situations that are complex and often messy, one activity they perform is to define a problem space: to name and bound a problem, the solution to which will improve their work. Sylvia Scribner (1986), who has conducted extensive study of thinking in the workplace, frames it this way:

> Skilled practical thinking involves problem formation as well as problem solution. Models of formal problem solving suggest that problems are "given" and intellectual work consists of selecting and executing a series of steps that will lead to a solution; the initial problem may be decomposed into subproblems as part of the solution procedure, but its terms are fixed. By contrast [our] studies suggest that expertise in practical problem solving frequently hinges on an apt formulation or redefinition of the initial problem. (p. 21)

Donald Schön, writing in *The Reflective Practitioner* (1983), similarly argues that for professionals, "problem setting" is central to their work:

> [Problem setting is] the process by which we define the decision to be made, the ends to be achieved, the means which may be chosen. In real-world practice, problems do not present themselves to the practitioner as givens. They must be constructed from the materials of a problematic situation which are puzzling, troubling, and uncertain. In order to convert a problematic situation to a problem, a practitioner must do a certain kind of work. He must make sense of an uncertain situation that initially makes no sense. (p. 40)

For teachers, this problem setting is rooted in their expertise. They frame problems based on what they believe students should learn and what they expect should happen in the classroom. Researchers on teachers' knowledge agree that this expertise comprises a combination of general pedagogical knowledge, subject matter knowledge, pedagogical content knowledge, knowledge of context, and knowledge of one's students (Ball & Cohen, 1995; Grossman, 1990; Shulman, 1986, 1987). Pedagogical knowledge involves knowing something about how students learn, and Shulman argues that pedagogical content knowledge is specific to teaching concepts vital to the teacher's discipline. It means that, in addition to having general knowledge about learning, English teachers know techniques for teaching writing, science teachers know how to teach the scientific method, and history teachers know how to help students grasp how societies change over long periods of time.

Teachers may be considered experts in their domain—learning, teaching, and subject matter—although it is clear that the degree of their expertise varies. Glaser (1984) summarized the findings of studies on expertise conducted with professionals in a wide range of fields as follows:

1. Experts excel mainly in their own domains.
2. They perceive large meaningful patterns in their domains.
3. They are faster than novices at exercising the skills of their domains, and they quickly solve problems with little error.
4. They have superior short-term and long-term memory with regard to their domains.
5. They see and represent problems in their domains at a deeper (more principled) level than novices; novices tend to represent a problem at a superficial level.
6. They spend a great deal of time analyzing a problem qualitatively.
7. They have strong self-monitoring skills.

If teachers formulate their pedagogical problems based on this kind of expertise, they must also do so based on the many contexts in which they work, including the school organization, policy environment, and community. Schön (1983) points out that the problem formulation process is not entirely a rational one, but is influenced by multiple factors outside the technical expertise itself:

> [Professionals] are coming to recognize that although problem setting is a necessary condition for problem solving, it is not itself a technical problem. When we set the problem, we select what we will treat as the "things" of the situation, we set the boundaries of our attention to it, and we impose upon it a coherence which allows us to say what is wrong and in what directions the situation needs to be changed. Problem setting is a process in which, interactively, we *name* the things to which we will attend and *frame* the context in which we will attend to them. (p. 40)

Teachers, then, formulate pedagogical problems to be solved based on a combination of their expertise and values. These values (what's important for students to learn, and how) are influenced by their personal experience, but also strongly by the culture of the school, and the values of parents and the surrounding community.

In our discussions, the five teachers from Woodland clearly linked their technology use to challenges they had experienced in their teaching. Like other professionals, they were able to focus their work through this problem definition. For Rob and David, it was the challenge of helping students to deeply understand Newtonian physics. For Peter, it was the problem of getting students to stay motivated and make deeply understood, significant connections between disciplinary fields. Joel wanted his students to break out of the box of traditional economics and begin to understand the complexities of real-life business; at the same time, he wanted his course to appeal to a wide range of students. Clarence wanted to teach students to write, to free up their process, to teach them that play, experimentation, and the option to discard were all valid parts of the process. And Clarissa wanted to be sure that her students never imagined running a business without technology as a ready tool for planning, marketing, record keeping, and analysis. For each, computers played a role in resolving an important challenge and supporting a vital goal.

## SCANNING FOR NEW IDEAS AND PRACTICES

Having defined these challenges very much in the way that Schön suggests, the five teachers naturally sought solutions to them. This process was supported by the open systems approach at Woodland, which allowed, and even encouraged, teachers to look outside the immediate environment for ideas. The culture of an organization with an open system promotes connections with people, information, and other organizations outside itself (Scott & Cohen, 1995). The five teachers I studied undertook a surprisingly varied range of learning activities related to computers over the span of many years. The school supported these teachers by allowing them the flexibility to guide their own learning, and provided support for choosing whatever forms worked best to help them develop, such as professional courses on content knowledge, the teaching of a subject, technology-based curricula, and cognition and learning. Some teachers took school- or district-sponsored workshops on basic computer skills or particular software applications; others taught such workshops. Some participated in summer-long or yearlong programs sponsored by corporations or universities. These programs helped them learn about the possibilities of technology for instruction, and often supported them as they attempted uses in their classrooms.

Clarissa, Peter, and Rob were very involved with subject-based organizations and networks, attending conferences and professional sessions, receiving grants, and staying in touch with their contacts by e-mail. Through these professional networks, they discovered new instructional ideas and models. Both Peter and Rob took sabbaticals at other educational institutions to work or study, which provided each with more in-depth exposure to the possibilities for computer use in classrooms. For Clarence, Clarissa, and Rob, experience in a degree program offered critical exposure to technologically integrated instruction and laid conceptual groundwork for their development of curriculum. New technical knowledge was obtained gradually by all the teachers over many years from all these various sources, but also by reading manuals, "just playing around," and seeking help from students, friends, and family.

With many different professional development opportunities from which to choose, what drove the teachers' choices for professional development? With instructional problems in mind, the teachers chose professional development opportunities that promised to be interesting and helpful. They engaged in experiences that interested them, and built knowledge and expertise over time. For example, Peter's interest in the classics pulled him to Tufts University, where he was introduced to a powerful hyperlinked database. After initially trying to use that database as an information source, he saw the potential of having students create their own hyperlinks, because creating a hypermedia presentation requires students to structure knowledge in a way that aids their learning of it. Similarly, with his background in lab work, Rob's visits to subject area conferences allowed him to see how computers could make labs more efficient, more exciting, more cutting-edge, and more powerful. A master's program in instructional technology helped him refine his thinking and design the classroom he wanted. Continued exposure and work with colleagues, including his coteacher David, helped develop a range of technology uses in the classroom.

Underlying this process of looking to diverse venues for resources, which I call *scanning*, is an intellectual journey in which teachers are deeply engaged with developing their subject discipline and pedagogy. And in this case, their ideas include an openness to using computers in the classroom. So, as they made their journey looking for interesting and helpful ideas, resources, approaches, and curricular materials, they also looked for what kind of technology might help them teach a scientific concept or an interdisciplinary connection. These are stories of intellectual growth. That growth was supported by the availability of resources from the school and district alongside recognition that the teachers were professionals with an intellectual life who were capable of navigating their own growth.

This approach, intellectual at its core, was enabled by school, district, and state policies that made professional growth, including the ability to engineer that growth, a required element for certification, recertification, and yearly evaluation. All teachers were required to develop professional learning plans in which they established goals for their own progress and planned activities to that end. At the school level, teachers developed these plans with supervision from the principal or another administrator and were required to design their experiences in line with the school's goals. This meant that the school principal could help shape the plan by coaching, but not mandating, teachers to try new experiences with technology or other instructional innovations. Ultimately, however, the course of professional learning was up to the teacher, which allowed room for intellectual growth and professional exploration.

## CREATING NEW CURRICULUM AND PRACTICE

For all these teachers, using computers effectively in the classroom involved creating new curriculum and classroom practice. For constructivist teaching with computers, there were no shortcuts through predesigned software packages, no matter how glitzy or sophisticated. For Rob and David, the backbone of the emerging curriculum was a series of lessons developed at a university, which they altered and augmented in significant ways. Clarissa's use of computers evolved in conjunction with the development of her Entrepreneurship course; essentially, they grew hand in hand. Joel could envision what he wanted to do with technology, and as the technology evolved, so did his use of it. Clarence's instructional approaches, patterns, and rhythms in the classroom were different because of using computers than they would have been otherwise; he created techniques to take advantage of word processing capabilities.

The key to the elusive process we call *technology integration* is to evolve the technological uses at the same time as, and intertwined with, curriculum and instruction. It is a matter of parallel creation. This is very different from the way we usually discuss this as "learning." The word *learning* implies that something already exists, which must be mastered. This is the wrong way to think about this process. Teachers learn about technology, and they learn about pedagogy or content. But the way they put it all together entails a creative process that combines received knowledge with newness, really the essence of professional growth. To say a teacher "learns" this might be a bit like saying an artist "learns" to make a painting. Some elements of technique are out there to be learned; yet others remain to be created anew by the artist.

For these five teachers, integrating technology essentially meant developing new curriculum and lessons—far from adopting any predeveloped package. The teachers created curricula to take advantage of what the technology could help with, such as research, presentations, data analysis, or simulations. Using the computers regularly often meant a shift in emphasis, perhaps toward assigning more independent projects to the students. Although teachers generally retained the topic outline they'd used previously and still emphasized key skills and concepts in the discipline they taught, introducing computers meant that the day-to-day instructional activities of teachers and students could change quite a bit. It would be difficult to say whether using computers for teaching takes more classroom time or less in the end, but it does undoubtedly reorder things.

In most cases, teachers created new curriculum and lessons one step at a time. Generally, they began with a unit or project, expanding from there, each year incorporating computers for longer periods and in more aspects of their work. As time went on, their use of computers became more routine and more intensive in increasing numbers of units and projects.

All of these teachers, however, kept some work aside from the computers. They still lectured, gave tests, had students read books, write research papers, and work interactively in groups. The computers, over time, simply became an important element in their instructional repertoire—not the only element. Thus they could not adopt a software application or curriculum wholesale. They had to make it their own, appropriate to their teaching styles and their students' needs.

## TRYING, REFLECTING, AND REFINING

The ability to take risks in the classroom, to feel as if attempting something new was a good thing, even if one faltered, was central to these teachers' work on integrating computers. This trying, reflecting, and refining was a smaller cycle within the overall learning process I am describing, one which was absolutely essential for the teachers as they developed their uses of the technology. This smaller cycle was at the center of their professional growth, the place where they figured out what worked and what didn't. It describes a continual refinement of instructional practice that never stops for the good teacher who is continually learning.

Trying something new in the classroom, with an "audience" of 15 to 30 young people, is nerve-wracking even to veteran teachers. Whenever these five attempted a new lesson using computers, they initially felt great uncertainty. They talked about beginning by "just jumping in" or adopted the attitude that they would just "learn right along with the students." There was always the sense that they needed to push ahead by trying it out, even when they weren't sure their new strategy would work.

Diving in provided them with data about how well their plans worked with actual students. After such lessons, they debriefed, so that reflective conversation with any available adult flowed naturally from the class periods I observed. Teachers would reflect on how well the computer use fit with the teaching goals, how well students understood what they were doing, how best to assess what they were learning, and what technical glitches arose that wasted valuable time.

Donald Schön (1983) helped define reflection in the professions by arguing that the work of the professional combines knowledge of models for problem solving within that profession with "an epistemology of practice implicit in the artistic, intuitive processes which some practitioners do bring to situations of uncertainty, instability, uniqueness, and value conflict." He further argues that "the workaday life of the professional depends on tacit knowing-in-action, which is the understanding of many aspects of practice which the practitioner would have difficulty describing" (p. 49). Schön continues:

> In his day-to-day practice, [the practitioner] makes innumerable judgments of quality for which he cannot state adequate criteria, and he displays skills for which he cannot state the rules and procedures. Even when he makes conscious use of research-based theories and techniques, he is dependent on tacit recognitions, judgments, and skillful performances. . . . [P]rofessional practitioners often think about what they are doing, sometimes even while doing it. Stimulated by surprise, they turn thought back on action and on the knowing which is implicit in action. . . . Usually reflection on knowing-in-action goes together with reflection on the stuff at hand. . . . As he tries to make sense of it, he also reflects on the understandings which have been implicit in his action, understandings which he surfaces, criticizes, restructures, and embodies in further action. (p. 50)

*Reflection-in-action*, then, is "thinking about something while doing it" (p. 54). In teaching, it involves the teacher's taking into account the many variables that come into play every hour in the classroom: Am I getting across the concepts I need to teach? Are the students learning? How do I know? How do I find out? How do I approach this subject matter to make it interesting and accessible? How do I deal with students whose prior knowledge or skills differ widely? Are students who are working in groups learning together, or are one or two individuals the only ones learning? Is the use of this technology assisting or hindering my goals? Is it taking up more time than it should? Does it confuse the students?

Schön describes an experiment performed with young children in which they were asked to balance blocks that had different centers of gravity on a metal bar. He points out that while the children proceeded by trial and error, *thinking-in-action*, as he calls it, the researchers attributed their learning to shifting theories about the properties of the blocks. It was the researchers, writes Schön, who needed the language to talk about what was occurring. The children themselves merely proceeded by testing the blocks with their hands, building a better and better sense of where to place them in order to balance. Schön reflects on the disjunction:

> Knowing-in-action which the child may represent to himself in terms of a "feel for the blocks," the observers redescribe in terms of "theories." . . . A conversion of this kind seems to be inevitable in any attempt to talk about reflection-in-action. One must use words to describe a kind of knowing, and a change of knowing, which are probably not originally represented in words at all. (1983, p. 59)

Similarly, the teachers I interviewed varied in the precision of their language when asked to talk about their classroom practice or their own learning. Yet from watching them and speaking with them, it was quite clear that they were highly reflective about their work.

Much like the researchers in Schön's study, I developed my own understanding of the teachers' reflective process, whether or not they themselves could articulate it. I believe that their pedagogical theories (how students learn and how teachers should teach) created the mental landscape against which they tested the reality of their teaching practice. These theories were different for each teacher. However, when they decided whether to bring computers into their classrooms, they made the decision, based on their prevailing theory whether it was worth the trouble. When, after each lesson, they reflected on how things went, they used the principles embedded within their theories to determine what aspects were successful, and where changes were needed.

Schön points out that a practitioner's reflection may not take place right away, arguing that reflection is bounded "by the zone of time in which action can still make a difference to the situation." For the teachers studied here, who remain committed to the school and teach pretty much the same courses yearly, this "zone of time" can stretch from the minutes that elapse between one class period and the next, all the way to knowledge and reflections accumulated over many years. In addition, adds Schön, reflection might take place on a wide variety of elements in a teacher's environment:

> He may reflect on the tacit norms and appreciations which underlie a judgment, or on the strategies and theories implicit in a pattern of behavior. He may reflect on the feeling for a situation which has led him to adopt a particular

course of action, on the way in which he has framed the problem he is trying to solve, or on the role he has constructed for himself within a larger institutional context. (1987, p. 55)

Schön also argues that practitioners may redefine problems as necessary, impose new frames when old ones don't work, or reflect on the understandings they have brought to the problem or their own role in it. Essentially the reflection-in-action described by Schön is a cycle between trying things in practice, building theories about what worked and what didn't, then pouring that research back into the next trial.

When someone reflects-in-action, he becomes a researcher in the practice context. He is not dependent on the categories of established theory and technique, but constructs a new theory of the unique case. . . . He does not keep means and ends separate, but defines them interactively as he frames a problematic situation. He does not separate thinking from doing, ratiocinating his way to a decision which he must later convert to action. Because his experimenting is a kind of action, implementation is built into his inquiry. (1987, p. 68)

This describes well the process of the teachers in this study, who invented new practices using computers, tried them out in practice, reflected on them over varying lengths of time, adjusted, then tried again. After each try, the practice was almost always refined, even if in minor ways. This is the process I call *trying, reflecting, and refining*. It is at the center of the developmental process by which the teachers created uses for classroom technology.

This cycle of trying, reflecting, and refining occurred over short and long periods of time, on issues of the smallest detail (such as seating or the wording of instructions) and of the largest sweep (such as including or deleting course topics or major projects). This process was at the heart of the teachers' learning. Without it, the commitment to use the computers, well-defined pedagogical problems, good access to resources, and creative ideas about technology integration would have had no impact on classroom teaching.

## RELATIONSHIPS AMONG THE FIVE LEARNING PROCESSES

It is important to understand these five learning elements conceptually as essential elements in the teachers' learning process. However, I do not propose them as stages in progression. In fact, they each reappear time and again as a teacher learns, linked to one another in smaller cycles. Scanning resources, creating new curriculum, and trying/reflecting/refining, for example, were often related in a cycle of their own. A teacher would describe how he or she needed a new idea, discovered one, tested it, and then refined it over time.

The characterizations I have developed will be most useful as a set of interrelated processes—concepts for understanding how teachers come to undertake high-quality teaching with technology. The very nature of this complex type of learning defies efforts to place it into a reproducible set of stages or a schematic with arrows pointing from one part of the process to another. Relationships between these elements of learning can run in any direction, and sometimes in smaller cycles that contain only two or three of the elements.

From the case study narratives, the reader should see the theoretical elements manifest in each case. Yet the cases also demonstrate that the teachers followed individual paths, even though they work in a common setting. These are powerful stories about connecting pedagogy with computer use, the history and learning of each individual, the centrality of subject matter when determining which computer applications to use, and how teachers coupled the possibilities of the technology to their pedagogical philosophies, curricular needs, and the needs of their students. The cases also demonstrate how these individual teachers developed over the years, and sets the stage for understanding how the organizational culture of the school promoted and supported their individual development.

# CHAPTER 10

# Completing the Puzzle: Learning and Organizational Culture

WHAT ASPECTS of Woodland's organizational structure and culture promoted this challenging learning? How did the school support teachers as they created new, constructivist uses of computers? The answer to these questions lies partly in the realm of the school's structure. In its basic structure and rhythms, Woodland was like most other high schools: It served a large number of students, whose course of study was divided into subject-area courses to earn Carnegie units; it had a four-period day on a block schedule; and teachers were organized into subject-area departments. But Woodland's teachers, unlike many others, had adequate time and space allocated for their work, a strong technological infrastructure, and opportunities to interact with colleagues and the school principal.

Even more compelling, however, were the answers that lay within the school's culture. Socially determined norms, values, and ways of thinking created a school where teachers' intellectual work was supported, but simultaneously shaped by certain boundaries. An enduring pride in autonomy was bounded by a focus on constructivist learning and a sense of accountability to the school and the families it served. The culture of Woodland High School created push-and-pull dynamics between encouraging innovation and expecting quality work. This applied to both faculty and students in a fascinating way that pervaded the work of the school.

Structure and culture make up the components of an organization, but they overlap to such an extent that separating them conceptually is sometimes counterproductive. The best ideas about learning and technology integration cannot be pursued when a school lacks structural resources such as money, budgeting discretion, or time for teachers to learn. On the other hand, the ideas that form the center of a culture can determine how structures are put in place. For example, the notion that continuous learning was important led this state, district, and school to create structures that required teachers to plan and account for their own professional development. A structure was created based on an idea.

Living within a particular structure for many years can shape one's thinking such that people come to consider the structure as "normal." A prominent example of this is the age-grade structure of most schools, which has become so deeply accepted that it is part of what we think of as school, and we would not be sure how to function without it. The concrete realm of structure and the ideational, social world of culture meld together. To handle this conceptual problem, I begin by analyzing the most concrete features of the organization that are relevant to teachers' learning: first, the technological infrastructure and, next, the availability of time, space, and opportunities to work with colleagues. I then describe the forms of professional development that were supported by the school, district, and state policies, and how the organization of offices, committees, and departments affected the life of the school. Finally, I discuss culture in its most ethereal terms: the central ideas that defined the norms, values, and thinking of the faculty and students at the school.

## THE TECHNOLOGICAL INFRASTRUCTURE

An organization possesses an "embedded skill" when a particular set of tasks or area of expertise becomes expected or taken-for-granted in the organization (Schein, 1992). For Woodland, the ability to maintain the technological infrastructure has become standard organizational knowledge, something that is embedded in the day-to-day life of the school.

Students and teachers at Woodland had very good—though not universal—access to computers. At the time this research was conducted, there was approximately one computer designated for instruction in the building per every four students. The majority of these machines were new generation computers. Almost all machines in the building provided access to the Internet as well as to an intranet system that provided storage space and e-mail for students and teachers. There were 16 computers available in the library, which was open from 7 A.M. to 4 P.M. during the week for students' use. Eight laptops were available for students to sign out overnight. There were enough computers for an entire class of students in two science classrooms, one English classroom, the Social Studies Department, the business classroom, and the industrial arts and design classroom. Teachers allowed students to use these computers even outside of class time provided an adult was available to supervise. I observed quite a bit of before-school, after-school, and free-period use of the machines.

Without exception, each teacher had access to a computer for his or her use. Sometimes the teacher kept the machine for his or her exclusive use, either in a classroom or office. In other cases, teachers made use of a computer in the classroom that was also available for students; since almost all computers were connected to a password-protected server, teachers could safeguard grades, letters, e-mail, and personal material. This easy and personal access to computers meant that teachers had the opportunity to increase their ease and familiarity with the machines. They were able to learn new software on their own, and use the computers on a regular basis for word processing, e-mail, and Internet research. E-mail was easily accessible, and virtually all teachers used it regularly. Most communication between administration and faculty was conducted by e-mail, so almost all the faculty logged on regularly, even if they preferred not to.

A central server provided personal electronic storage for students and teachers throughout the building. Access to individual accounts on the WHS server meant that students always knew where to find their work. It remained secure and available at all times from almost any computer in the school. The system manager performed backups once a week, so that if the server crashed or an individual student had trouble finding a file, the work was still available.

Some problems arose from the fact that both PC's and Macintosh computers were used at Woodland, and sometimes attempts to transfer documents between home computers and school were met with difficulty. If a student had produced a piece of work on a PC, it might be difficult to transfer it to a Macintosh, or vice versa. Few teachers had the expertise to make conversions between all formats. The technical support people did have the expertise and necessary software, but would become overwhelmed if they were approached each time this occurred.

Yet the flexible culture of the school made this problem manageable, even if it took time and energy that people would rather have used elsewhere. Students caught without the platform they needed could head to the library or another lab to find the necessary computer, or might get permission to leave the classroom to find one of the technology staff to help them. Students were trusted to continue their work, even if they had to leave the classroom. Most students seemed to figure out a system for their own work after a while: how to transfer files from their home computer to various classrooms.

WHS made a clear commitment to technical support by dedicating two full-time salary lines to support personnel, one whose responsibility was to manage the network, and another who functioned as a troubleshooter. The network manager maintained the connections between all the computers in the school, the server, and the Internet hub in the building. Many schools assign these tasks to a teacher or administrator with other responsibilities, or have a consultant develop the network, then call that person for help when something goes wrong. What this generally means, in practice, is that kinks in the network system accumulate, frustrating teachers and students trying to use it, but no one is contacted until the entire network crashes. Then it may take several days to repair it. This kind of downtime will keep teachers from venturing to use computers for teaching, because it makes planning impossible.

The teachers at WHS told me that they generally have some kind of backup lesson plan in case the computers don't work. However, the constant attention paid to the network by a specialist meant this did not happen very often or for very long. During the year I spent at WHS, I observed or heard about three network crashes. Two of them were fixed within several hours; one took about 24 hours. Another example of how such technical support is essential to successful instructional use arose when teachers and students began to find the Internet access in the building too slow. In the beginning of the 1997–98 school year, an insufficient number of IP addresses meant some difficulty accessing the Internet, usually a slow response. After this was identified as a problem, Jimmy, the network specialist, had the skills and budget to find a solution, which was applied within weeks of identifying it, easing the problem.

Ned was the second technical support person at WHS. Since he had fewer formal qualifications than Jimmy, the school was able to pay him at a relatively low rate. This cost-saving strategy was what enabled WHS to afford the services of a second full-time technical support position. Ned's primary responsibility was to help staff and teachers at the school with the range of technological problems that emerged over the course of a day. He was available to teachers practically on demand, and was also accessible to students who had questions about such issues as e-mail or file conversion. Ned was constantly on the move, responding to one issue after another. I saw him rescue teachers from the kinds of problems that occur in the middle of a lesson. System software might crash; a configuration file could turn up damaged or missing (causing a glitch in Internet access); the printer network could stall out; or students might have trouble accessing the server. When problems like these occurred during class time, instead of feeling isolated or frustrated, teachers called Ned. More often than not, he managed to be available.

I noticed that Clarissa, the business teacher, seemed to call on Ned quite a bit during her classes. I asked her specifically about his role in assisting her. What she said captured nicely the importance of having troubleshooting assistance available on demand:

> I can't imagine teaching with technology without Ned, because there are some days that either I'm not comfortable enough problem-solving through what's happening, or I've tried everything, and I still can't figure it out. Or I just don't have the time. I'm in the middle of a class, and something is happening, and I need some help. I'm sure that without Ned the amount of downtime with students would be

much greater. And there are fair stretches where I never have to see him, and then there are fair stretches, where I ask for his help a lot. He usually comes right up when I call. He's always right there. He's great. We're very lucky to have him. And he's great with the kids. . . . They are comfortable approaching him. He's very supportive too—I can bounce ideas off of Ned, and he's very supportive, and then will go and find me the stuff that I want to play around with.

During this year, WHS also decided to hire a half-time person to provide additional support for teachers trying to learn to use technology in the classroom and to support the work of the technology committee. They hired Rob, one of the teachers featured in this study.

The technological system is run in a way that treats teachers as its clients. The teachers and the technology professionals work together to formulate what is needed by the teachers and in the classrooms, based on how the teachers think about their work. The technology staff then tries to meet those needs. Woodland has become so good at providing technological infrastructure that this expertise fades into the background as standard organizational knowledge, something the school simply knows how to provide. This is an important lesson for other schools, that the technological backbone should be set in the background, not the foreground, of the organization.

## TIME, SPACE, AND OPPORTUNITIES TO WORK WITH COLLEAGUES

Outwardly, Woodland looked like a typical comprehensive high school. Over 1,000 students in a large building studied a curriculum designed to get most of them into college. This was supplemented by various electives, which included the usual music, drama, and art, as well as academic electives and some community service. WHS was a relatively accommodating place to work as faculty. Four periods of classes were scheduled per day, with A-days and B-days alternating. Depending on the whether it was an A or B day, teachers had between 90 minutes and 4 hours preparation time per day, far more than teachers have at many schools. There was plenty to do during preparation time: work with students, grade papers, carry out administrative tasks. Even so, the time available left teachers less frantic and pressured than they would be at a typical school. This was very important, in that it allowed them more time to explore instructional innovations such as technology.

Teachers had desks and office space separate from their classrooms. The configuration of these spaces determined which colleagues they interacted with most often. All teachers had office space with a desk, shelving, a computer, printer access, and, in most cases, a shared phone. These were generally cubicles within larger offices, creating open, shared working space. Classrooms were usually shared by several teachers, so the majority of faculty were anchored in their offices, where they kept their books and papers, and often met with students. When I asked teachers which of their colleagues they spent the most time with, they uniformly referred to their office mates.

In 1991, when the offices were constructed, teachers were assigned to them in a way "intended to promote interdisciplinary conversation," according to the principal, or "in order to break up the departments," according to some faculty. But several teachers related that over the previous few years, faculty have shifted around the offices in ways that tended to put teachers of common subject matter back into shared space—and indeed this arrangement was evident.

I expected this subject-area grouping to have implications for the kinds of conversations held between teachers, that perhaps working next to a colleague in the same department would lead them to have more conversations focused on pedagogy and teaching. And although teachers who did not share space with others in their academic department said they thought they could talk more about teaching if they did, in fact those who did share space with other department members told me they tended not to talk about instruction, pedagogy, or curriculum very frequently. Rather, those sharing office space conversed about issues with particular students or about life at the school. Most told me that they discussed curriculum and teaching issues with colleagues from other schools who teach the same or parallel courses, rather than with those from their own school who teach different courses. The academic departments did meet to discuss curriculum issues, which, due to the introduction of the Vermont Frameworks the previous year, were a central focus.

Another structure within which teachers interacted was through the many standing committees at the school. These provided multiple avenues for interaction with colleagues on issues of importance to the whole school, and created a sense among the teachers that they had a voice in how the school was run. The multiple committees helped teachers to be professional, to take on roles outside the classroom, and created a very important sense of community and interchange. Teachers were expected to participate actively on at least one committee of their choice. These committees coordinated many of the school's activities, or at least gave advice to the administration on how to run them.

The Technology Committee was an important one; its role was to lead the development of technology use in the school. It did some purchasing, addressed technical problems, posted and filled any technology-related positions, and strategized how to promote further use. In addition, its existence had symbolic value: Having a technology committee signified to the school community that technology was something worth paying attention to. Those who sat on it were the leaders in developing classroom technology for the school. The collective expertise of the committee was high, and each year they developed and implemented a technology plan for the school, which was backed by the administration and funded by the school's board.

Another important committee was the Graduation Challenge Committee, which made decisions about how the process would work. This committee's activities included reviewing the requirements of the project and the assessment rubric for the paper or presentation, monitoring the pass rate, and discussing issues that arose, such as deadlines or possible plagiarism.

An additional committee was the Curriculum Clearinghouse, which established and ran a procedure for all faculty who sought to introduce new courses at WHS. This committee sponsored a detailed application process for any new course, with opportunity for feedback to the teachers who proposed the course. And each spring, the Hiring Committee began its work to establish which vacancies had to be filled, set out a screening procedure for applications, and interviewed candidates.

The committees provided multiple opportunities for teachers to have a voice in running the school and to interact with faculty outside their department. Since the committees dealt with essential functions, and everyone sat on at least one, teachers at WHS had the opportunity for significant input into at least one area of the school's work. Teachers uniformly reported that although final decisions related to running the school were the principal's, she accepted quite a bit of input. She was perceived, by most, as a principal who listened to feedback and the opinions of the faculty, then made sound decisions. WHS staff also prided themselves on being able to speak their opinions, and for the most part, I did not find a climate of fear, but rather one of openness. Out of the many interviews I conducted, I did speak with one teacher who felt her opinions were ignored and seemed quite unhappy about it. She was, however, the exception.

These cross-cutting features of the school organization provided opportunities for teachers to feel empowered and involved with running the school. Teachers might be involved as members of the community or as active parents at WHS or a feeder school; they might contribute to departmental or committee work, voice opinions during schoolwide faculty meetings, or address the principal or administrators directly by conversation or e-mail. There were multiple opportunities for input, and they were encouraged. This was a lively, opinionated, extremely active faculty. While staff commented that all the activity made for a very demanding workload, they rarely complained about not having a voice in important decisions.

Departments also had discretionary budgets, as did teachers for individual courses. Departments generally used their budgets for professional development, equipment, books, or technology. Each teacher was also allocated a course budget, which could be used for field trips, class speakers, or for equipment and instructional resources. In some cases, there was enough money in a course budget to purchase additional technology. The fact that teachers could purchase computers, peripherals, and software through departmental and individual budgets as well as through the school-level technology budget is another example of how multiple structures at WHS provided teachers with considerable flexibility in developing their courses and teaching methods. This was an essential feature because it allowed the teachers to formulate a vision—to create the new instructional uses—and then purchase the materials to make it happen. The idea of a course budget is quite an unusual one, but plays a very important role because it gives the professional teacher the ability to make decisions about what materials are needed in the classroom.

## NORMS, VALUES, AND IDEAS: THE ESSENCE OF CULTURE

Some readers may be surprised to learn that the most essential cultural features that fostered constructivist teaching with computers at Woodland had little to do with technology. Rather, a shared pedagogical worldview, a strong focus on students, and the value placed on continuous learning and innovation combined as powerful elements to foster professional learning of all types, including learning about technology. In addition, an organic, home-grown sense of accountability was the glue that ensured professionalism and quality.

Although WHS teachers operated with great autonomy, the organizational culture provided underlying values and a common sense of what was favored in the organization that directed their work. Principles that fostered continuous professional learning and high-quality teaching were reinforced at multiple levels of the organization. As such, several unstated but nonetheless abiding normative themes were at the center of life at WHS as it related to the work of teachers:

- Learning is at the core of what we do.
- Our pedagogy is student-centered.
- We maintain autonomy and respect for the individual.
- We are accountable to the community.

These themes signify enduring and powerful social forces that guided the many decisions people made daily. They were at the center of the culture, yet existed at multiple levels much as a fractal contains large representations built from smaller pieces of the same pattern (Morgan, 1997). Such central values are simple enough to allow people in the organization to enact them in the way they do their work, the environments they build, their relationships, and the symbols they create and accept (Weick, 1995). While each theme may be understood separately, the four must also be understood in relation to one another, as a system with component parts working together. Here, I will describe each one of these themes in depth before going on to discuss how they interact.

## Theme 1: Learning Is at the Core of What We Do

Continuous learning was a natural part of life at WHS. A reader may be skeptical of this statement because the term *learning organization* has become so popular for describing schools, districts, or other educational units. At WHS, however, learning was a norm without a name, a process, or a grant attached to it. Teachers and staff came to expect that their work would proceed as a continual building process in which individuals and the school collectively shared responsibility for working toward improvement. It was a strong expectation that became a norm for those who worked there. New teachers were not hired unless the Hiring Committee could see in them a predisposition for continuous learning.

Learning was valued throughout the organization. The assistant superintendent—who had a strong influence on technology use at the school—was highly reflective, as was the principal. Both could tell stories of what they did in the past, how it evolved, and what was learned from it, then use these stories, in turn, to steward new projects. Apparently, the district and school board that employed them for over a decade were comfortable with their style of moving ahead through innovation and trial, building success one step at a time.

The administration valued teachers' learning by promoting openness, fostering innovation, supporting teachers' efforts to learn new practices, and allowing for mistakes to occur without punishment. This is reflected in the patterns I described earlier regarding how the five case study teachers learned to teach with technology. Each narrated a trajectory of learning that involved defining instructional problems, looking for new ideas, creating new curriculum, and testing and refining classroom practice, all elements consistent with research on adult learning in the workplace (Schön, 1983; Scribner, 1986). What surrounded this pattern—or was perhaps behind it—was that adult learning was valued by this organization, and the learning was allowed to occur in ways consistent with what we know about how adults learn. Being able to define instructional challenges requires a culture in which teachers do not need to hide the fact that they have questions about the effectiveness of their practice.

The working environment at the school was an open one, in which teachers were largely content, but disagreement with the administration was expressed when it existed. Although many faculty were glowing about the school, and most seemed happy with their jobs, several expressed strong conflicts with, or even disparagement of, the principal. Often during interviews, an otherwise contented teacher would critique a particular policy. Whole-faculty meetings were not tense, but did often entertain conflict. Overall, I found the faculty and staff at WHS did not fear the principal; they did not fear repercussions from any criticism they might pose. Several, in fact, sought me out to make sure I heard what they thought. This created a cultural environment in which open discussion of issues was allowed and teachers felt free to explore difficult issues in depth and raise challenging critiques.

Through the faculty committees and the principal's consultative style of leadership, teachers learned to address the problems of the school with one another. Through these committees they developed strong collegial relationships. The openness of the culture made it possible not only to define problems, but to take risks solving them; and this extended to classroom life. Teachers told me how much innovation was valued; no teacher ever expressed regret at having attempted a new practice. Beneath it all was tacit support for continuous learning.

Edgar, a veteran teacher, described how he understood what the school stood for in this regard:

> I think the school values—as an institution and in terms of the [kind of] leadership people want—they value the new. They don't value the old, like things that are perceived to be traditional, although I think that's beginning to change a little bit. . . . So people who are coming in here and wanting to impress the leadership would not be traditionalists, not people who necessarily value law and order, complete management kinds of people. Rather they should be people that embrace frameworks, standards, authentic kinds of assessment, constructivism—a lot of things that are now in the current view of education. But I've been around a long time. That radar will turn. In a few years, there will be a different set of terms.

It was clear that innovation and new ideas were valued at the school, even as this teacher expressed skepticism about the value of constant change.

Learning to use computers in the classroom was a form of innovation that was considered very important to the school, yet it was still not mandatory. Using new technologies fit well into the overall picture: They should be used because they are good tools for learning; they are on the cutting edge; and they support instructional innovation.

Academic learning was also stressed to students as being the central purpose of the school. They saw the work of their teachers as guiding their learning, not defining it. Of course, not all students behaved as if learning were central, and clearly the school's faculty and administration struggled with some students on issues of motivation and discipline. Still, walking through WHS, I generally saw students going about the business of school: attending classes, doing homework, writing, or doing research. The norm at WHS was to be serious about learning.

One of the most powerful elements of WHS's culture was that the value placed on learning applied to both adults and students. Seymour Sarason, in *The Predictable Failure of Educational Reform* (1990), talks about how adults must have the same positive learning environment as students if educational reform is to work:

> From their inception our public schools have never assigned importance to the intellectual, professional, and career needs of their personnel. However the aims of the schools were articulated, there was never any doubt that schools existed for children. If, as I have asserted, it is virtually impossible to create and sustain over time conditions for productive learning for students when they do not exist for teachers, the benefits sought by educational reform stand little chance of being realized. (p. 145)

For teachers, this culture that valued learning supported their intellectual life, opened the school to many resources, promoted innovation in the classroom, and did not flinch as teachers experimented. Clarissa told me,

> I feel like you're really encouraged to be innovative. You're really encouraged to try different things. And I think you're really respected for being the professional in the field that you were hired to teach. I do have the control, and I do have the freedom to kind of research and try different things.

Peter described the positive expectations for innovative teaching and maintained that WHS differed from most schools in this regard:

> Here, there's a recognition that you're "edge people." You are way out in front of everybody else. You are going to be out there and going to make mistakes, and [you] are going to have successes. And you're the ones who really need to be supported, because you have to accept the fact that not everything you're going to do is going to be successful, rather than playing it safe. I think that's the biggest difference here.

Edgar provided this perspective on the innovative norm at WHS:

> Everything gets promoted ultimately. In the past, it was promoted through the principal. . . . Whatever the idea is, you would go through the principal or have some contact with her. And it would go. I can't imagine any kind of a thing here that a faculty member might be interested in doing that wouldn't have a moment or two in the sun. And I think probably 95% of ideas that have been generated—course ideas or activity ideas, or things that you want to do, try, pilot, whatever the case may be—[are] very much encouraged. Nothing is discouraged here. It used to be just because that's the way the principal was. I think it's a little less so now, because there seem to be more hoops that you've got to go through. But I still think it's fairly open-ended in that you can go someplace and hear something that's there that might be interesting. This school, in all the years that I've been here, has always been known for innovation. I think sometimes to its detriment, just in trying too many things. But that is sort of the credo of WHS. If you've got an idea and want to try it out, do it. And most often, if there's an idea someplace that helps out in education, somebody here in this school is going to pick it up, and they're going to try it at some level.

Clarence summed up the feeling of being able to try new things by saying, "I think it's very safe here." And Joel compared his experience at WHS to what he knew about other places: "Very few schools allow the experimentation that goes on here to a large degree."

Expectations about continuous learning were linked to expectations that teachers would be innovative. Innovation was fully expected from teachers, and those who were best at it seemed to thrive, obtain support for projects, and receive positive recognition.

The culture around learning at WHS was strong partly because of school leadership and partly because of its roots in the history of the institution. What makes it particularly powerful is that a pedagogical perspective sits at the center of it. Having a philosophy about learning and teaching at the center of the culture is strongly appropriate for a school where learning is in fact the core function. It is similar to running a business in which customer service must be at the center. Such a successful business would position the satisfaction of customers so centrally that it was reproduced at all levels and in many places. So it is in respect to learning in a school. If learning is at the core of the culture, repeated in the manner of a fractal—many times in order to make a whole of the same shape—it can take many different forms for both adults and children.

## Theme 2: Our Pedagogy Is Student-Centered

A second important theme in WHS's culture was its focus on students. This value could be observed in many decisions made by school staff: how priorities were set, how time was spent, what was insisted upon, and what was let go. Being student-focused is a good way to describe a common pedagogical perspective shared by all the teachers with whom I spoke.

I chose WHS as the site for this study because during my initial visits I found quite a few teachers who undertook the kind of teaching I sought for this study: constructivist pedagogy using computers as tools. Over time, I found that the school's leadership did not explicitly use the term *constructivist*, nor did most of its teachers, even though instructional formats generally built factual knowledge and concepts first, then had students develop understanding through problems and projects. After a while, I came to label the prevailing pedagogical approach at the school *student-centered*, because this more general term seemed to better describe the work of these teachers who used similar techniques, yet had different ways of articulating their thinking about it. *Student-centered* signaled a general approach toward students and an orientation toward the many decisions made daily by school personnel.

Several organizational theorists argue that metaphors within cultures are powerful tools for understanding how organizations work and how people within them think about their participation (e.g., Martin, 1992; Morgan, 1997; Rossi & O'Higgins, 1980; Smircich, 1983). Through discovering a root metaphor, one can identify an organizing principle that characterizes what is really important in an organization. Root metaphors, according to these theories, are powerful symbols that are understood by participants to guide their actions, and represent their most important values.

At WHS, this root metaphor appears to be "doing what's best for kids." My first inclination upon hearing this phrase was to dismiss it as a piece of rhetoric, an official line, the kind of thing educators feel they must say they're about. But over time, I began to see that this phrase was repeated not only with frequency, but in connection with many decisions made by administration and faculty: courses, curriculum, interactions with students, school climate, and expectations, to name a few. Understanding "what's best for the kids" as a root metaphor connects myriad aspects of the culture of the school that would otherwise remain disparate. The power of this metaphor is worth exploring, without denying that adults at this school—as at any other—also serve their own interests, even as they struggle to serve the interests of students. The metaphor can be helpful; at the same time, it should not be engaged naively, as though all decisions were only made for children.

"What's best for the kids" signified the climate of student-centeredness at WHS. I came to understand that this phrase expressed the central pedagogical approach of the school, a pedagogy that encompassed not only instruction, but the staff's overall approach to creating a positive learning environment for students. It represented a set of norms that determined how teachers were hired and socialized, how they developed courses, what expectations they had of students, and how they conducted their work with students.

Most teachers took this emphasis on students to mean they had to pay attention to each student's learning, try to leave no one behind, allow opportunities for students to address their own interests, and provide tools for each individual to learn. In practice, WHS teachers employed a variety of methods to accomplish this: lecture, research, writing assignments, and presentations—almost always capped off by at least one significant independent project in each course. It also meant that teachers made themselves available to students seeking individual assistance. This is an important norm, which I never saw violated: any time I was speaking with a teacher or observing one, he or she consistently responded to students' needs. WHS teachers conceived of learning as a process each student essentially had to tackle on his or her own, by practicing concepts, working through difficulties, making connections to prior knowledge.

Although few teachers explicitly used the language of constructivist pedagogy to describe this process, their philosophy essentially lined up with the constructivist approach to learning. Although the language they used to describe their teaching was unique to each, and their techniques varied, in the end their instruction was based on the assumption that students work to build their knowledge as individuals; therefore, each student must be assisted somewhat differently.

In courses they ran, WHS teachers were especially sensitive to students' responses to curriculum, activities, and teaching style. For elective courses, teachers interpreted enrollment as an indicator of how popular the course was. In teachers' conversations about the market value of courses, they generally assumed that high-quality, challenging, interesting, relevant courses would have sufficient enrollment. If enrollment in a particular course was low, they should revise the curriculum or teaching methods, or else it would soon be canceled. Teachers told me repeatedly that a poorly subscribed course would not be considered a "good" course. This reasoning, this framing of what constituted a "good" course, signaled an attention to clients—defined as students and their parents—that prevailed throughout the culture of WHS. This is very different from a culture in which teachers think they know best and interpret students' reactions as resistance or laziness. It contributed to the student-centered atmosphere at the school; teachers thought of themselves as serving interests defined by students, their parents, and the larger community.

Joel summed it up this way:

> The real test is if kids are getting stuff out of the course, and they
> want to do it. If there's nobody in a course, it is obviously not doing
> well. You can tell by the kids. Some courses people have to take. The
> electives are where most of my time is spent. That's the ultimate test.
> Then they pass it on to their siblings, and their parents support them.
> That's partly how I evaluate a course. It's from the parents, and it's
> not formal either. I get encouraged when the kids keep taking the
> courses, and that's a sort of an evaluation itself, for me anyway.

Another facet of this student-centeredness may be informed by recall-
ing *The Shopping Mall High School* (Powell, Farrar, & Cohen, 1985), which
states, "If Americans want to understand their high schools at work, they
should imagine them as shopping malls . . . [which] attract a broad range of
customers with different tastes and purposes" (p. 8). That courses were continued or discontinued at WHS based on popularity demonstrates that the
school was committed to pleasing clients—students and their parents—and
even to marketing the courses in ways that maintained enrollment. Although
students at WHS behave more responsibly than at many schools, teachers
still noted that their real commitment to academic engagement varied: Some
did little work; others were in it only for credits and grades; still others worked
hard and exhibited genuine interest in learning. Pleasing some clients meant
making some or most courses sufficiently rigorous. Many students and their
parents were looking forward to entering college and needed to be well prepared. Responsiveness to students and parents meant that the teacher should
push hard, but not too hard.

The student-centeredness of the culture worked alongside the learning
focus to create a school that paid attention to its core function: teaching and
learning. The emphasis on learning—for students and adults—at WHS created an environment in which people knew what was important; the emphasis
on student-centeredness provided direction for that learning. These two elements combined to create an environment defined by social norms more than
by rules and regulations. Together they provided a shared sense of the school's
identity and ultimate mission, which Schein (1992) argues is "one of the most
central elements of any culture" (p. 56).

## Theme 3: We Maintain Autonomy and Respect for the Individual

A third fundamental strand that ran through WHS was the sense that teaching is an autonomous pursuit and that the needs and ideas of individuals,

whether teachers or students, should be respected. Teachers at WHS, as in most high schools, functioned with bottom-line autonomy within their immediate sphere of work. No matter what good work was done in committees or academic departments, the teacher's essential responsibility was to work well within the classroom. WHS teachers had considerable flexibility when planning curriculum and instructional strategies, within the guidelines of relatively loose state requirements for courses, students' needs for college entrance, and the established norms around student-centeredness.

Teachers wielded considerable decision-making power regarding curriculum and teaching in their own classrooms. They had enormous flexibility when it came to shaping curricula for their courses. They were always, of course, bound by the conventions of their subject and the expectations of colleges and parents, so teachers addressed these when planning topics for a core course like physics, algebra, or U.S. history. However, even within college preparatory courses, teachers had considerable flexibility with regard to the time they spent on topics and the depth with which they were treated. For elective courses, they could develop their own curriculum within the topical framework they initially described for the course. In all cases, the teacher chose the instructional approaches for any given course. All in all, teachers at WHS had considerable professional freedom.

Descriptions of personal and academic freedom, coupled with support of their work by the administration, arose repeatedly with teachers when I asked, "What's it like to work here?" The teachers conveyed a strong sense that the instructional process was fully in their domain, and the school generally a supportive one for teachers. The autonomy teachers felt contributed to a sense of power and responsibility over their own work, as well as enthusiasm for pursuing teaching ideas that meshed with their personal intellectual life. Joel described his feeling about it in this way:

> I like working here. There's a lot of academic freedom. They let me create what I thought was best, and for me that works well. And they support the kids. One way or another there's always been enough money I think to get the job done. They put the money where it's needed, and where the teachers think it should be. This school has a long history of teachers doing for themselves. There are very, very independent teachers in this building. They don't want much in supervision or direction. I don't think they could handle it if there were. A long, long time ago there were department heads and all sorts of structure, and that's the way a lot of schools are now with a very rigid departmental structure. It has its benefits, but also the cost is that there's very little creativity happening, because it is so narrowly defined.

Another teacher, who taught even more years at WHS than Joel, said much the same, highlighting autonomy as a key benefit for her:

> I just love it here. I think I like it because of the freedom, and it really is a climate that is stimulating. There is just about every resource here, whether it's human or whatever, so that if you have a question, or you have something you want to look up, or bounce an idea off someone, it's available here. I think having freedom and being comfortable here is maybe the best way to describe it.

Autonomy and individualism does, however, have its flip side. One teacher—one of the ambivalents regarding technology whom I interviewed for the study—commented:

> In terms of being a teacher here, you have a lot of personal freedom. You don't have to answer to anyone about curriculum, which is good if you're a teacher who's conscientious. If you're not, it could be a problem. It's a very difficult school for new teachers to come into because you don't get support. There is no director. There's no head of the English department. There's a lack of communication between English teachers. And that can be great, because you can be alone and just do your own thing. But it can also be a problem, because it would be helpful to talk to each other and find out what we're doing.

Joel said this sense of individualism among the faculty developed over many years:

> We went through some really tough times [before the current principal arrived] when we were changing principals every 2 years. I think the people who have been here a long time became very, very individual and self-sufficient. That's why they are in some areas hard to deal with. They really won't—they don't—take direction very well here, because that's the way we moved through the system. We had to take care of ourselves. So if you have sort of been on your own for 20 years, you're going to develop strong ways to do things. It's pretty hard to break that. And that's good and bad I suppose. Anybody will tell you that who's ever tried to come and work with the faculty here. It's a hard faculty to work with. Because it's so ruggedly individualistic.

A first-year teacher echoed her more experienced colleagues:

Everybody's got sort of their own way of doing things and so everybody likes to be able to do what they want to do. The teachers here are very intelligent, I mean, they get top of the line people applying here, you know, for a number of reasons. Part of it, I think, may be that freedom, that academic freedom.

Even with all this emphasis on individualism, the school hung together as a community. I observed much of what I considered high-quality teaching, and the democratic governance structure ensured that parents were satisfied as well. How did the school culture promote individualism and innovation, yet at the same time ensure quality?

## Theme 4: We Are Accountable to the Community

Every organization, including every school, presents a public face: what the school articulates as its mission and goals. These may be considered its "espoused values" and "formal philosophy." These express what the school purports to be about, how it means to represent itself, and often what it strives for. The handbook and Web page for WHS describe the school and its mission, expressing important values for this school and the community it serves:

*ABOUT OUR SCHOOL*

Welcome to Woodland High School. We are committed to providing students with the best environment in which to grow and be challenged academically, and to pursue activities which make high school a special time. It is our goal, as the WHS community, to help students develop the skills, behaviors, and knowledge necessary to become contributing members of both the WHS community and the world community. We do not require students to elect a prescribed curricular track such as college preparatory, general academic, or vocational. The program elected should reflect the interests, abilities, and needs of each student. We encourage students to enroll in the most demanding program possible. This will allow the choice of various paths—college, job training, etc.—after the successful completion of high school. Guidance counselors provide each student with assistance in self understanding and in the selection of courses both yearly and on a long-range basis. Teachers and counselors help students understand the course offerings and provide recommendations as to appropriate student choices.

*OUR MISSION*

We believe that every student can demonstrate the behaviors, skills, and knowledge essential for a contributing member of a democratic society. The mission of WHS and the community is to ensure that learning for all students can challenge them to develop excellence in their individual pursuits.

The school put forth this mission to signal its commitment to providing a quality educational experience for all students and its philosophical opposition to tracking. Such documents should always be viewed as a public representation, the reality of which should be scrutinized, but they are important as symbols to which community, students, and faculty can refer in order to create some common understanding about the mission of the school.

The faculty and staff shared a sense of accountability for these goals that was developed over time within the school and was tightly linked to the expectations of the local community. Abelmann, Elmore, Even, Kenyon, and Marshall (1999) would call this a system of "internal accountability," because it was shaped by forces organic to the school and the community it served. They contrast such internal accountability to an "external system" that might be imposed from the outside by the state or another agency.*

The norms of accountability at WHS were powerfully embedded in the faculty's links to the larger community. For example, the average experience of staff listed in the annual report of 1999–2000 was just over 13 years, ranging from zero years experience to 34½. Although these numbers reflect total years of teaching experience (not only at WHS), and some people may have lived outside the local community before teaching at WHS, they still can be considered a rough estimate of longevity in residence. Most teachers I spoke with at the school grew up in the state, had lived there many years, and planned to remain. Faculty members had their children in school at WHS and its feeder schools, were active in community activities, were involved in school board elections, and might easily meet up in the grocery store or in the ski areas. This small-town feel and the love many staff felt for living

---

*This analysis was strongly influenced by the paper cited and by discussions with the Harvard-based staff of the Consortium for Policy Research in Education during 1996–1998, regarding theories of accountability. The group included Richard Elmore, Leslie Siskin, Charlie Abelmann, Susan Kenyon, Elizabeth DeBray, and Katie Woodworth.

in the area fueled a commitment to the life of the school beyond paid professional responsibility. Many teachers told me that although they might consider changing careers, as long as they continued teaching they would not want to teach anywhere but WHS.

In addition, the governance structure for schools in the state required that each school have its own board, and that the union district also have its own board drawn from those of the elementary, middle, and high schools in the district. The WHS board alone consisted of 11 people. Each year people in the towns that sent their children to the high school voted on its budget. These structures, plus local newspapers and numerous informal networks, created an atmosphere in which the community was quite involved in the life of the school.

Inside WHS, accountability was shaped by the expectations of students and their parents. The norm of accountability was strengthened by the norm of student-centeredness, which required that teachers pay attention to students and their learning; satisfy students with interesting, rigorous courses; and satisfy parents with evidence that students were happy, learning, and able to successfully enter college or the workforce. The strong pull of the community on WHS teachers served to make them accountable for one of the things most valued there: the student-centered approach.

Accountability was linked to the norm of individualism and autonomy as well. Joel Westheimer writes, in *Among Schoolteachers* (1998), that "individuality and community are unexpected bedfellows" (p. 145), as he discusses the nature of professional community in two schools. Westheimer argues that individuality and community exist side by side when individuals "gain (rather than lose) a sense of identity and individuality through their participation in the community" (p. 146). He describes a culture in which individual achievements are how one wins respect and admiration from the community, and teachers take on roles as strong individuals or "characters." At WHS, individual accomplishments—and sometimes collective accomplishments—were an important way to win respect and to satisfy students, parents, administration, and the local community. In other words, through individual accomplishment, WHS teachers fulfilled the expectations held for them. The most important accomplishment at WHS was to develop a reputation for quality teaching.

At WHS, a teacher's reputation rose or fell in relation to his or her knowledge of subject content and pedagogical expertise, ability to reach students, the popularity of courses, and feedback from students and parents. This is not to say that teachers at WHS did not work in teams or did not see their school as a whole, but rather that a teacher's reputation in the classroom—and the satisfaction of his or her students—was clearly more important than anything else.

Quality teaching emerged repeatedly as the most important way to gain the respect of the administration and faculty colleagues at WHS. "I think that if you're a good teacher," one member of the faculty told me, "you're important to the administration." Teachers were quite focused on maintaining or improving the quality of their teaching. My visits to offices and classrooms showed teachers with reference books at hand, buried in curriculum materials, busy grading papers, or working directly with students. A first-year teacher, when asked what she perceived was important to building a good reputation as a teacher at the school, described what would be considered quality, professional teaching at WHS:

> Creativity, self-motivation, and really high level thinking are pushed by the administration. Getting students not just to be able to regurgitate back and find places on the map. I mean while that's important and we want to be able to do that, we also want students to think about the big ideas, and think about how knowledge relates in their lives and relates to other . . . disciplines.

Clarissa talked about what she felt accountable for in teaching: innovation, quality, and keeping current.

> The people who don't like teaching don't stay here. Because it's a hard place to teach, I think. [No one tells you,] "This is what you're supposed to do and how you're supposed to do it." You're responsible for deciding that for yourself. . . . You're expected not to teach the same thing in the same way, year after year after year. You're expected to stay current and thrive. And there is a strong push for that.

This flexibility gave teachers a feeling of power, independence, of being professionals respected by their employer. In my conversations with teachers, I also sensed deep respect for one another's work. The same first-year teacher quoted above described her feeling about working at WHS:

> Excellent, excellent teachers. I think just intelligent people, too, and willing and able to communicate that intelligence to the student population. Here, it comes down to hard work and intelligence, demonstrating that you are really committed to making the best possible classes and making the best learning happen in your classroom.

One way to frame this quality in Woodland's teachers is to use the term *professionalism*. WHS teachers certainly possessed a rather special sense of it. Writers about educational policy frequently decry the absence of professionalism in teaching as a major problem for the field, comparing teachers' status, privileges, and core knowledge unfavorably with, for example, doctors and lawyers. Linda Darling-Hammond's (1997b) definition of a profession is that its members share a knowledge base defined by the profession and assume responsibility for developing that knowledge among their members through education, licensing, and peer review. A profession is self-regulating in that it educates new members to use standards of practice that put the interests of clients first, and to base decisions on best available knowledge (p. 298). "Public confidence," Darling-Hammond continues, "is warranted only when a profession has ways to continually expand its knowledge and when it has specific methods of ensuring that the people it admits and allows to practice can be relied on to possess that knowledge. . . . [Professionals use a variety of strategies] to ensure that decisions are *client oriented* and *knowledge based*" (p. 299).

Literature that describes teachers as professionals assumes that they must possess deep knowledge of subject content and pedagogy, in order to manage the complex interactions between themselves, content, and students during the learning process (Ball & Cohen, 1995; Darling-Hammond, 1997a; Lieberman, 1988). Teachers, in this conception, base their instructional technique on knowledge and experience, reflecting constantly on their actions and the effects these seem to have had on learners (Schön, 1983).

Teachers at WHS saw themselves as professionals and were treated as such by the school and district leadership. Being a professional at WHS meant accepting responsibility for the learning of students, responding to their requests and needs, working hard in the classroom and on committees, interacting thoughtfully with colleagues, and staying current in one's field. In a culture that stressed individualism it also meant taking individual responsibility—grasping that the bottom line for a teacher's work was what happened each day with students in the classroom. Teachers felt responsible for developing high-quality, innovative curriculum and instruction. Their sense of accountability for these practices provided an important piece to the puzzle of why teachers were able to learn difficult new practices at this school.

WHS's teachers saw responsibility for good teaching as the natural companion of the autonomy and academic freedom they experienced. Clarissa described the system of accountability at WHS that makes the privilege of autonomy dependent on good instructional judgment and a high level of responsibility:

There isn't this monitoring, this "turn in your lesson plans every Friday so they can be checked out by a department head" kind of feeling. At the school I taught at before here, there was more of that. The department head was always checking your work. "What are you teaching? What do your units look like?" There's not that here. At first it's frightening, because there is no one making you accountable. I really value that here. The principal says "do whatever," as long as it's educationally sound and you feel it's the right thing to do.

So, while teachers realized they had considerable freedom and treasured it, they also knew that with that freedom came responsibility for self-direction, innovation, quality control, and continuous learning. At WHS, that was part of the pact.

Accountability was also connected to the value placed on continuous learning. At WHS, it was assumed that teachers would continue to learn about their subject area and, secondarily, about new teaching techniques. Teachers understood their continued professional learning as necessary to their work at the school. Through the five case studies presented earlier in the book, I have already illustrated the many ways teachers learned at WHS. It is important to realize that this was a cultural norm: teachers perceived that continuous learning was part of their job and integral to their work as professional educators. Not only the five case study teachers but all the teachers I spoke with made it a routine part of their activities to attend conferences, to take courses, and to continue reforming their teaching practice.

## NOT A FORMULA: CULTURAL COHERENCE, CONSISTENCY, AND APPROPRIATENESS

These particular cultural constructs would not work in every setting. Their ability to guide the work of the school's faculty arises from their coherence as a set of principles, their consistent use over many years, and the contextual appropriateness of the culture within its community. Along with sustained leadership at the school and various supporting structures, these cultural ideas, norms, and values created an environment in which WHS teachers could create complex instructional practices, including those that used sophisticated technology. The four themes of the culture—learning, student-centeredness, individualism and autonomy, and accountability to community—worked in concert to balance individual motivation and creativity with a pedagogical focus and a sense of accountability for quality teaching. These elements of culture were rooted in strong traditions of the wider community and history of the school and sustained by the district and school leadership. The leadership provided resources, pedagogical direction, and shaped standards for what would be considered quality work.

These cultural elements shaped life at WHS. They influenced every action taken and decision made. Individualism and accountability to community counterbalanced each other; they allowed each person to pursue individual learning within boundaries that favored development of the whole. Learning at the core describes an overall attitude that infused administrative and teaching decisions, while student-centeredness guided the type of pedagogy adopted, and how quality was judged by administrators, teaching colleagues, students, and parents.

The culture of WHS developed over time. Its tenacity is explained by the strength and longevity of its leaders, who come from the larger community, and the consistency of the culture with the values of that larger community: independence of thought, hard work, and seriousness.

WHS was founded in 1964. As one of the first "union" schools in the state, it drew from smaller districts to create a large, comprehensive high school. Its purpose was to save money and provide a wider range of curriculum choices for students. At that time, its founders had the opportunity to consider what kind of school they wanted.

In the following quote from the principal one can see layers of history: the value placed on learning, decisions that center on students, respect for the individual, and accountability to community. The principal's consciousness and understanding of these elements allowed her to lead by embedding them in her daily work. Here she begins by talking about the founding of the school:

A decision was made that money would be put into teachers and teaching. And they went out and looked for teachers under the motto "Excellence in Teaching." The main idea was that teaching was not passive. Learning was not passive. It was a passion. And so they went out and brought in quite an innovative faculty to start this building. The tradition has been one of maintaining a very different approach. A more progressive approach. As it relates to pedagogy, it is grounded in the tradition of, "How do you create opportunities for learning?"

So there's a long history that has been nurtured here, cultured here—which is not the traditional "sit down and take notes" kind of thing. There's a culture here. From the kids. From the parents. And from the community that says, "Here's the type of approach to learning that we believe is important." So I will tell you, a very traditional teacher coming into this setting—and by "traditional" I mean [a teacher] who has the students sit down and lectures to them, gives only written tests—would not make it culturally. Kids would have trouble with it. Colleges may have trouble with it. And probably that individual wouldn't make it through the hiring process. So there's been that culture here. If you can figure out how to do something in the best interest of kids, we'll try and support it.

Many teachers had used similar words independently. "What's best for kids," "what's in the best interest of kids," were phrases that came up repeatedly during my conversations with teachers, and led to my formulation of that idea as a central metaphor for the organization. I asked the principal about it.

> INTERVIEWER: "The best interest of kids." . . . Does that mean something here? I mean, people in almost any school would say they do things in the best interest of kids.
> PRINCIPAL: I think what it means is very different here. You look at the individual. Their individual growth is what's important. And the challenge that we're having now with the new state standards frameworks is how do you continue to have kids grow and yet also hold them to standards? The real issue is how do you balance the human need to learn and the idea that learning doesn't take place in a standard environment? Here, I think, people will talk about how you look at the individual in the context of the community, rather than the community making the individual conform to that context.

## MOVING BACK TOWARD THE CENTER: ORGANIZATIONAL CULTURE'S INFLUENCE ON PROFESSIONAL LEARNING

Woodland High School created an environment for teachers' learning that encouraged intellectual exploration, innovation, and risk. The leaders of the school hired good people, then supported them as they did their work. High-quality, constructivist uses of technology developed as part of teachers' continuous learning about new techniques and pedagogies. Technology use was backed by a stable but flexible infrastructure that was treated as a service for professionals. The prevailing ideas of the culture were continuous learning, innovation and quality, student-centeredness, and autonomy. Quality was ensured by way of the inner controls of the school and through an internal social and cultural system that made teachers accountable to parents and the broader community through the students they served. The lessons to be drawn from this school are fairly complex; they involve understanding how the interplay between structure and culture leads to each reinforcing the other to promote the goals of the school. Leading in this way requires a kind of artistry, a sense of balance, and weaving together various aspects of leadership.

When technology becomes an integral, expected piece of the work for everyone involved, it becomes part and parcel of this system. It becomes something teachers think about pedagogically, something that is supported with resources, something that is expected by students, parents, and school boards. However, to fully integrate technology into classrooms, it must also be fully integrated into the conceptual leadership of the school, particularly with its core function, instruction. Technology and pedagogy must be inextricably intertwined, so that the use of the first grows along with the development of the second. Supporting this requires an attitude that promotes learning and exploration, and tolerates mistakes. It requires a culture that keeps its important ideas at the center of the work and reinforces those ideas through symbol and action at every possible level. Quality instruction, with technology, sits at the center of the picture; the professional learning of teachers is required to get there; and the organizational culture must support this teacher learning in a way that simultaneously allows for intellectual growth and risk, but shapes teachers' work at the service of the school and its students.

# CHAPTER 11

# Recommendations for Leaders

THE FINDINGS of this study have important implications for policy and leadership, some of which apply in a general sense, shaping learning environments for teachers, and a few of which are specific to fostering the use of computers for constructivist teaching. I have framed them in the form of lessons for leaders, whether at the school level, state or district policy level, or within communities.

Out of the findings of this study, I would like to offer several recommendations to educational leaders. I begin with those that are more specific to fostering technology integration.

*Understand that the best technology use will be rooted in sound pedagogy. Keep pedagogy front and center.*

Technology added to a pedagogical approach that is unsound cannot produce good instruction. Computer-based technology—or any other kind of technology—cannot in and of itself improve instructional practice. If technology is added on to poor practice, the teaching will continue to be of poor quality. Some educators seem to believe that purchasing expensive software packages will supersede a teacher's incapacity in the classroom, or will introduce new, powerful instructional paradigms.

What this study clearly shows is that teachers take curriculum resources such as software and *create* uses for them. Those uses tend to be extensions of the teachers' existing theories of teaching and learning. Each of the teachers in this study found possible uses for computers and brought them into the classroom through a complex and creative process of rebuilding curriculum. The teacher is always the driving agent when it comes to technology use. In this study, the pedagogical theory held by the teacher drove his or her use of technology. Although in some instances, powerful technology-based curriculum or other experiences on the road to learning about the technology affected the teacher's thinking, it was always the teacher's agency that determined the quality of classroom use.

*Urge teachers to use classroom technology through norms, not requirements.*

From a teacher who is a dedicated professional, the commitment to bring an innovation into the classroom is of tremendous value to the organization. With that commitment comes the kind of intellectual focus, energy, and motivation to succeed that cannot be mandated. In this study, teachers committed to using computers once they were convinced they would be a valuable tool for teaching. Good professionals will adopt technology only when they see a pedagogical reason for doing so. Once Woodland faculty were won over by its teaching value, they willingly undertook the extra effort required to learn about the technology and create uses for it.

Providing valuable technological and professional development to teachers who are not won to its purposes can mean wasting it. The norm of autonomy at WHS meant that teachers did not feel they had to pretend to adopt computers. Yet, in many schools, an attitude toward innovation that stresses compliance may lead teachers to spend energy to look like they are using the computers, when in fact they are just going through the motions. True commitment means teachers will be focused on learning and creating high-quality instruction. Seeming committed on the surface is not enough.

*Make technological and material support a predictable constant.*

For the teachers using technology successfully at WHS, access to computers and stability of the technological infrastructure was a dependable feature of daily life. This meant that they had access to a satisfactory quantity of computers during class time (as defined by the teacher), that the computers worked almost all the time or were repaired quickly, that the networks for storage or Internet access were stable, and that troubleshooting help was readily available. Though the system may not have been perfect, its essential stability meant that teachers could plan their lessons and, on most occasions, complete them without tripping over technological failure. It meant that they did not spend undue energy dealing with access and breakdowns, and it meant that they did not have lesson after lesson fail to meet their own and their students' expectations because of network outages or machine failure.

Having access and stability as a constant fuels teachers' commitment to developing uses for computers. It frees them to focus on the instructional aspects of the work, rather than jockeying for access or readjusting plans because of breakdowns. Technological instability saps teachers' energy from the most important work at hand: creating high-quality instruction. As professionals, their expertise is best employed when they are free to teach.

One of the great strengths of the organizational system at WHS when it came to promoting technology was that the infrastructure was so solid and consistently maintained that it was accepted as a given. In a way, it faded into the background; it was usually not a primary concern. This allowed the teachers to focus on teaching.

The technology personnel treated teachers and students as their clients, working at their behest to support instructional needs. The goal of a school wishing to promote classroom computer use should be to provide technical support as a service to teachers and students so that teachers can focus their energy on what's important and what they do best.

*Accept that learning to integrate computers takes lot of time, and that the best uses will be locally created.*

Teachers at WHS who used computers most successfully began using the machines during the 1980s. High-quality instruction that takes advantage of computers as tools takes considerable time to engineer and refine. University professors who develop curricula and software that they transport to schools have certainly applied a lot of time and expertise to the instructional design. Adopting such a program, in partnership with university support may take less time than developing it within the school, but still the teachers must learn to use the program in their own classrooms, and the program itself will require adjustments as it is used with real students.

Faculty will require considerable time to learn hardware and software—whether that software is curriculum specific or a more general application. For example, a social studies teacher who would like to employ spreadsheets for data analysis in a sociology project has to learn basic hardware operation, the main concepts of a spreadsheet, and the specific application available to the school; master advanced functions such as charting and graphing; figure out how the spreadsheet might fit into a project and develop the project, and structure lessons for students so they can learn to use the program well enough to analyze their research data. It's a lot of work, and without a large block of time in the school year to accomplish it, the most likely scenario is that a teacher will learn the necessary skills and develop a unit slowly over the course of several years. This is what I observed in all five case studies of accomplished technology users at WHS.

*Open the system. Accept expertise.*

When it comes to technology, considerable expertise is likely to be found outside the school. A significant advantage held by Woodland's organization was its open systems approach, which allowed many outside influences to seep through the organization's barriers. In practice, this meant that faculty and administration participated in a wide array of professional activi-

oltz et al., 1997). So that I could observe teachers learning to
s as tools in teaching, I needed a school that had moved past
ases of technological adoption. In addition, the school site for
to be a place where faculty were struggling to make their peda-
ach authentic for students, based in real-life problems, so that
vely constructed knowledge.

having these qualifications were quite rare. I sought nomina-
king to a wide variety of people about the requirements for the
ing national organizations involved with technology and learn-
partments of education, and individual educators. I visited a
hools, but all were either too early in their technology adoption
cable providing liberal access to a researcher. Finally, a contact
ional School Boards Association led to the nomination of the
e WHS is located.

his particular school based on a theoretical sampling strategy
ies (Glaser & Strauss, 1967; Patton, 1990), because it was a
upplied an "opportunity to learn" about the object of the re-
, 1995). To determine what characteristics were most critical
to be studied, I followed the example of two previous studies
Melmed, 1996; Means & Olson, 1995) that also examined
are relatively rich in technology and promote project-based,
t learning. I knew that the school I chose should have suffi-
to technology to allow at least lead teachers to grapple with
the technology in their teaching (Becker, 1994; Glennan &
96; Means & Olson, 1995; Sandholtz et al., 1997; U.S. Con-
. Such a school was difficult to find. I contacted many people
owledgeable about schools and technology to try and find a place
equirements of the case study. I contacted schools in six differ-
l visited potential sites in Massachusetts, New York, Texas, and
ally, on the recommendation of a former principal in New York,
he National School Boards Association, and was introduced to
der in Woodland's area. I visited, discussed the study with the
erintendent, and then toured several schools in the district.
ined this school's suitability for the study through several pre-
rs with the technology coordinator, by interviewing the princi-
e teachers, observing four classrooms, and attending an Internet
hrough this process, I determined that teachers at WHS had good
hnology for teaching, that the school had systems to provide
upport and maintenance, and that many teachers were using
hnology in their classrooms. The four teachers whose classrooms
e all using constructivist pedagogy. Preliminary interviews with
s and with the principal confirmed that WHS teachers widely

ties from diverse sources, including universities, professional networks, participation on state- and national-level committees, conferences, workshops, and even part-time assignments. At WHS, this open approach was routine: Information on opportunities was circulated, and taking advantage of the opportunities made easy because time and funding were provided. This attitude led to a very rich pool of ideas among the faculty.

*The best teachers are intellectuals.*

To say that teachers at WHS were treated as professionals would be only part of the story. It is every bit as important to note that their intellectual life was lively, part of the day-to-day fabric of the workplace. The faculty were generally people who took their subject disciplines seriously, kept abreast of new developments, had opinions about them, and thought hard about their work in the classroom. In a monograph written by Henry Holmes in 1937 called *Shall Teachers Be Scholars?* he made the following argument:

> Scholarship [is] a major defense against formalism in teaching. A teacher who really knows enough of his subject to teach it and has, besides, a broad professional outlook, will resist the pressure to make himself a mere drill-master. Subjects that are to live in the minds of the young and have any vital effect on their acts and attitudes must be taught by those who know them well. . . . Sufficient scholarship among teachers thus appears as an indispensable factor of educational and of social progress. (p. 17)

Material and cultural support for intellectualism among teachers fosters empowerment and creativity: the best of what they can give in the classroom.

*Policymakers in states and districts should be aware of the necessity of consistency and coherence in culture. They should value and sustain strong, stable leadership, and they should consider the value of new leadership paradigms.*

When policymakers frequently change leaders and policies, they interrupt a sense of stability and cultural consistency that is required for intellectual work and classroom innovation. They should be aware that such changes may have significant impact on the work of a faculty. For this reason, they should attend carefully to the implications of policy changes for the consistency and coherence of school culture.

At WHS, we saw that the culture worked well partly because its pieces held together well: They interacted in ways that made up a powerful whole. That whole fostered learning, creativity, and development of quality instructional practice. It was also an appropriate culture, organically connected to its place. It built on local history and traditions, and extended honored traditions at the school. The consistency, coherence, and appropriateness of the culture, combined, gave it its power. Policymakers should tread carefully when making policies that upset the work of leaders and faculty who are doing the slow but steady work of building the culture necessary for a quality school.

## Me

THIS STUDY was designed to examine
grate technology into constructivist te
tional context supports or fails to sup
I combined several qualitative approa
processes that occur within individuals,
environments. This appendix will descr
study, including general approach, sam
vation protocols, data organization, ar

The work of Michael Patton (1990
egies for sampling and data collection.
ducted according to "purposeful strateg
(p. 176). Patton writes, "The logic and
selecting information-rich cases for stu
one can learn a great deal about issues
of the research" (p. 169).

To study the learning and organizat
puters for constructivist teaching require
watch this learning. Patton describes thi
cases that are rich in information becaus
fest the phenomenon of interest intensel
amples (p. 171). Toward that end, I sough
any special grant and not participating i
gram, either university-based or corpora
teachers and students had sufficient acce
ers could focus on learning, rather than o
fixed, or learning the fundamentals of
sought had to have used technology for
with sufficient technical support. The m
stages of awareness and concern for mana
working to implement technological innov
density of teachers struggling with the simp

1987; Sand
use comput
the initial p
the study ha
gogical app
students ac
    School
tions by sp
study, inclu
ing, state
number of
or uncomf
with the N
district wh
    I cho
for case st
school tha
search (St
in the sch
(Glennan
schools t
construct
cient acc
how to u
Melmed,
gress, 19
who wer
that fit t
ent states
Vermont
I contact
a district
assistant
    I de
liminary
pal and
worksho
access t
technol
compute
I visited
these te

used this approach, and that teachers were at various stages in their learning to use technology in teaching, from beginning to advanced.

The principal permitted me access to any committee meeting and any teacher in grades 10–12.* The faculty were friendly and willing to talk with me throughout the year. Collection and analysis of data had two strands: teacher learning and organizational context. I obtained four forms of data pertinent to my research questions: school documents, formal interviews, informal interviews, and observations of classrooms, meetings, and school life. I obtained documents relevant to school structure, curriculum, course and graduation requirements, and work on committees or in departments. *Formal interviews* were "arranged meetings in bounded settings out of ear-shot of other people" (Hammersley & Atkinson, 1995, p. 139), lasting approximately one hour, and using an interview guide developed in advance (Bogdan & Biklen, 1982). They were audiotaped and transcribed, including analytic and interpretive notes in the transcriptions. *Informal interviews* occurred in classrooms, hallways, offices, the faculty room, or the library.

To obtain this data, I spent 6–10 days per month visiting the school throughout the academic year, and took up part-time residence in the community. From each day's observations, I recorded field notes, including interpretive notes and themes for follow up.

To study teachers' in-depth learning, I chose five teachers who became the subjects of case studies. This number was large enough to provide several cases of rich learning, and small enough to take a close look at each teacher and the organizational elements that affect that teacher's learning. To find candidates for these case studies, I obtained names from the principal, technology coordinator, and teachers in each academic department in a "chain-sampling" procedure (Patton, 1990, p. 176). I then determined which teachers satisfied certain conditions listed below by conducting a screening interview and at least one classroom observation. Each teacher I selected took a constructivist approach to teaching, as defined by the following features:

- Teachers acted as coaches for students, helping them build mental frameworks for knowledge.
- Skills and knowledge to be taught were embedded within projects or themes that were meaningful to students.
- Students' ideas were important in classroom life; knowledge was understood as collaboratively constructed by students and teachers.

---

*Grade 9 at WHS is called the "Core," which works as a team to provide an academic and social foundation for students entering the school. While I requested permission to study these teachers as well, the principal felt that they were too busy developing their own work to spend time with a researcher.

- Assessment was frequent, providing helpful feedback to both teacher and student, who act on the results of the assessment.
- The teacher taught metacognitive skills as part of the curriculum.

In addition, teachers chosen for case studies told me that they planned to use technology actively for teaching throughout the year, and in new ways. These conditions ensured that the five teachers I studied would likely be actively engaged in learning throughout the school year. I chose teachers who taught in different subject areas, so the five were associated with four different academic departments. All the teachers expressed willingness to participate in the study.

Classroom observations grounded my discussions with the teachers about their learning. I observed at least 10 class sessions of a single course taught by each teacher to provide continuity, focusing on lessons in which teachers were expressly using technology for teaching.

Before the sessions, I explored with the teachers their goals and methods for each lesson: what they wanted students to learn, how they thought the lesson or project format would help students learn it, and how technology would assist the process. These questions prepared me to observe the lesson, as well as providing information about the teachers' beliefs and theories about teaching. During classes, I made detailed notes on the teachers' activities, students' activities, and how computers were used. Often following these class sessions, I was able to converse briefly with the teachers, asking them to reflect on how the class went.

## THE INTERVIEW PROTOCOLS

Information from these observations laid a basis for three formal interviews with each teacher, during which I asked about: (1) the history of their professional background and how they learned to use computers in the classroom; (2) how they thought about their teaching, basing my questions on what I'd observed; and (3) and how they understood the school organization in which they were working.

To gather information on organizational structure, culture, and leadership, I interviewed the principal, technology coordinator, and at least one non–case study teacher from each department regarding the culture of WHS. I asked about their perceptions of how space was used, how students were grouped, teacher's schedules, class assignments, and department and committee structures. I also obtained information on what support structures existed related to technology, such as technical support, placement of computers, access, and the governance of budgets. I then asked what they thought were the most important values for the school and the most salient professional norms (e.g., what is valued here?).

I have provided sample interview protocols on the following pages. These protocols were constructed with a semistructured interviewing technique in mind (Bogdan & Biklen, 1982), as guides for conversation, notes about what I wanted to know, and the development of precise wording prior to the interview. I created them based on the conceptual frameworks and prior research I have discussed above. For example, to find out how teachers learned to use classroom technology, I attended to—and prompted for—what skills, knowledge, and beliefs they might mention. To understand their learning processes, I asked for and paid special attention to information on individual study, reflection, or inquiry. However, I often found that the framework of concepts with which I began was too limited. As it should, the research process expanded my understanding and complexified or made problematic some of my prior categories. For example, I would never have anticipated the incredible array of learning activities these teachers undertook, nor the subtle links between professional norms and community accountability. This school was such a pleasure as a research site partly because teachers and other staff were quick to counter my assumptions.

In order to understand what elements of the organizational culture may deter teachers learning to use computers, and understand the reasons why some teachers choose not to use them, I interviewed teachers at WHS who do not use computers for teaching. This provided information that served as a counterpoint to what I found by focusing on teachers who were actively learning to use computers.

All structured interviews were taped and transcribed. I produced notes from more informal conversations as part of daily field notes. In addition, I gathered considerable documentation from the school and from teachers in the study, including annual reports, self-study documents, surveys, and curriculum materials.

I obtained additional information on the school culture with regard to adult learning through extensive observation of meetings, informal interactions, and just hanging out. I attended at least one meeting of each department, as well as several meetings of the school and district technology committees.

Sample interview protocols follow.

## First Case Study Interview: Learning History

- How long have you been teaching?
- And how long have you been at WHS?

- Tell me a little bit about your educational background.
- How would you characterize what you learned during those experiences (each one)?
- How did you learn to use technology in your teaching? (Explore formal and informal learning opportunities.)
- I'm interested in hearing your general philosophy toward teaching, how you approach it.
- What is your philosophy about teaching with technology?

### Second Case Study Interview: Based on Classroom Observations (Rob Trace)

Protocols were designed for second interviews specific to each teacher. As an example, I have provided below excerpts from my questions from the second structured interview with Rob Trace (see Chapter 4), taken from a transcript of that conversation. The following are the questions I asked. Many refer to work I observed in the classroom.

- I'm going to begin by asking you about some history, and then ask you to talk some about what I saw in the classroom. Before you began using computers, what did your classroom look like? Did it look very different than it does today?
- What did your classroom look like when you first began teaching?
- How has it developed over the years?
- In response to what?
- Thinking back to that early period of teaching, were there things in the classroom that made you think about shifting? I sense that you developed a more constructivist approach over the years, and I'm curious about how that shift occurred, particularly in terms of challenges that you saw come up in the classroom.
- At one point you told me that you looked at the results of tests. That's the kind of thing I mean—not whether you looked at the literature. As I remember, in the early years of teaching, so many challenges come up, and you start to think: Well, how do I face these? I'm trying to get you back to that time and ask if this evolution in your teaching had anything to do with responding to those kinds of challenges.
- What about that period was formative?
- The demonstrations—you mean classroom demonstrations? That's something I haven't seen you do this year, so how did that change? Why?
- The Physics Teachers Association conferences—do you stay in touch with people you meet there?

- You showed me a master of the packet that you use, that you give to the kids, and that you make notes on during every unit for when you change it the next year. What are some examples of things that you either changed this year, or are going to change for next year?
- [Following up] What were the students overwhelmed by?
- Why did you decide to focus this year on getting the students to produce multiple representations?
- Based on that, what will you do next year?
- So by the time they handed in their labs and did the other forms of assessment that you use, did you think they grasped what you were trying to teach?
- So they do a midterm that involves labwork that's similar to what they've been doing. How does that feed into what you'll do after that? I mean, if you find a kid who's clueless, what does that lead you to in the next month or couple months?
- A few minutes ago, you were talking about how much you guide them versus how much you let them figure things out themselves. I'm really curious about that: How do you choose when to tell a kid what's going on? I saw students struggle hard with some of the physics concepts, particularly at the point in between the labs and problem solving—you could really see the wheels going. "What is this velocity thing we're talking about?" So, how do you decide where and how to intervene? If somebody's stuck, how do you decide?
- Somebody calls you over, and you have decide, you have to diagnose the problem. What goes through your mind when, let's say somebody asks a question and it's clear it's not the technology or the software—it's a Physics question. How do you decide how much to help, or how much to push them to do it on their own?

## Second Case Study Interview: Based on Classroom Observations (Peter Marcaz)

Below is the interview protocol I drafted prior to my second structured interview with Peter Marcaz (see Chapter 5). Its purpose was to explore how Peter thought about teaching. Some of the questions listed are repetitive and were only asked in one form. However, writing them out in advance helped me understand various possible angles from which I could pose a question.

- Where did you get the idea for the philosophy assignment? Why use the Web? What does it add?
- What were your hopes for what the students would learn by making the Web pages?

- What about this assignment appealed to you?
- Would you do this one again next year—why or why not?
- Would you make any changes? If so, what would be the nature of the changes, and why?
- Can you identify particular students for whom the activity worked well— or not? [how he thinks about pedagogy in relation to students]
- How did you decide on or create this assignment?
- What benefit do you think students get from making links to other sites?
- How did you learn how to make these Web pages yourself?
- How did you think of these ideas for the last two assignments?
- What is your purpose or goal for the curriculum in using the Web or in using hypertext?
- What happens if a kid doesn't see a benefit—how do you talk about that? [how he explains worth]
- What made you decide to insist that students do Web pages in the second project?
- What are some of the problems you've encountered in your teaching? What are some of the issues or struggles you've faced?
- What have been the most difficult components? How do you face those difficulties? How do you problem-solve around them?
- What are the most rewarding components of teaching for you?
- What's the most important part of this unit—the philosophy project?
- What would you do differently next time?
- How did you decide that those were the things?
- What do you want students to know at the end of this unit that they didn't know at the beginning? Is the computer knowledge part of it? [get at his thinking about this assignment]
- What kind of teaching do you think will get them there?
- What parts of your teaching support those outcomes, and what about your teaching doesn't support them quite yet?

**Organizational Interview**

This interview was conducted with the five case study teachers (as their third interview), and other teachers in each academic department, including ambivalents and nonusers.

*The Adoption and Use of Technology: Values, Supports, Impediments*

- How important is using technology here?
- What happens to those who use it?

- What happens to those who don't?
- What at this school helps people use technology in the classroom here?
- What do you think are the barriers or problems that get in the way of people using it?

*Learning Opportunities*

- How do people learn about using technology here?
- How do teachers learn new teaching practices here?
- What do you consider good teaching practice?
- Where do you go when you need help with something that has to do with your teaching? Let's say you're trying to figure out how to work with a particular group or students, trying to do more group-based activities, or trying to figure out how to teach writing.
- What do you talk to your colleagues most about in the course of a day?
- How about instruction—where and when, if at all, do those conversations occur? What are they about? Give an example.
- Probe: departments? offices? teaching teams?
- If you had to name one group of people on whom you most rely for help in instructional matters, who would it be and why?
- If people have drifted back toward departments in offices, why have they done so? What are they seeking?
- How do you learn about new teaching practices here? Tell me about anything you've done in the past year that has led to your learning something new.
- Where do you go when you need help with something that has to do with your teaching, especially an "instructional puzzle," something you're trying to learn to do better?
- If you are working on a lesson or a unit using technology, and you're trying to figure out how to make the whole thing hang together, where do you go for help?

*Organizational Values: Exploring What Teachers Perceive Is Valued*

- If someone were just coming to teach here next year, and they asked you, What do I need to do to impress the administration here? what would you say?
- What would you tell them to do to impress their colleagues?
- Who are the most influential people at this school? Why do you think they are influential?
- What kind of activities get promoted around here? What kind don't?

*Exploring How Teachers Characterize the School, Themselves, and
Their Colleagues*

- What's it like to work here?
- How would you characterize this school compared to others you've worked in or are familiar with?
- What kind of teachers teach here? How would you describe this faculty?

## Interview with Ambivalents and Nonusers: Use of Computers and Beliefs

This interview was conducted with teachers who used computers less or not at all in their classrooms.

- Please tell me how you use computers in your classroom, if at all.
- If yes, why use them? Under what conditions do you use them? If not, why not?
- What would convince you to use them?
- What supports would you need to help you?
- What would you need to know to be able to use them?
- What classroom management skills do you think you would need?
- What technology management skills would you need?
  *Explore*:
  - *Beliefs*
  - *Skills*
  - *Knowledge*

## Interview with Principal on Professional Norms

This is a sample protocol from an interview with Woodland's principal.

*Themes*

- Definitions of good practice
- Definitions and norms of professionalism
- Norming—how norms are established and maintained
- Professional evaluation

*Self-Improvement Norms, Professional Standards*

- There seems to be a strong norm for self-improvement among the teachers I've talked with here. Do you specifically promote this? If so, how? If not, how do you think it comes about?

- What do you define as good teaching practice?
- What do you look for when you go into a classroom?
- You've said that you will soon begin to expect that all teachers use technology as a classroom tool. How do you plan to enforce this?
- How has it worked up until now? Clearly, a good number of teachers are using technology. Do you think they're doing that just because they want to or because they see it as valued in the school?

*Creating Norms and Values: Accountability and Culture Management*

- How do you reward people here? What do you reward?
- How does someone get fired here? Can you tell me a story without using names?
- What do you expect teachers to use their prep time for? Are there instances where you need to speak to anyone about it?
- What are teachers accountable for? Who holds them accountable?
- As for you, how do you judge what they're doing?

*Learning Opportunities*

- What is your philosophy about setting up learning opportunities for teachers?
- What is your policy about conferences? What is your policy regarding conferences and subs?
- Sabbaticals?
- Under what circumstances do you answer no when someone asks to attend a conference or go off on a sabbatical?
- How do you balance decisions about spending resources on professional development specifically for technology versus other types such as content?
- How do you insure that the technology use has quality? Who decides what quality is? How is it decided?

*Other*

- How often do you get to see teachers teach?
- Should I talk with other administrators?
- You seem to be pursuing some kind of restructuring. Tell me about it.
- What do you see as the purposes of the various committees? Do they relate to teachers' learning? What will happen to them?
- How do you think about planning professional development for the year? How do you measure and weigh the different possibilities? How do you decide whether it's been effective?

- Who decides what will be done in the course of a year?
- What role does the Individual Professional Development Plan play? [This was required by the state.] How do you decide what to accept in a teacher's plan? What role, if any, do you think the plan plays in teachers' learning? What part does their fulfillment of it play in their evaluation?
- What part does continuous learning play in their evaluation?


## DATA ANALYSIS

I coded and analyzed data throughout the study. While I was "sensitized" (Patton, 1990; Strauss & Corbin, 1990) by the concepts I laid out earlier, the literature I have reviewed, and my own experience, I also developed theories and increasingly refined conceptual models about my research questions throughout both the data collection and analysis phases. Ongoing analysis guided subsequent data collection (Hammersley & Atkinson, 1995). During fieldwork, I wrote analytic memos to identify themes, puzzles, or contradictions in the data, and to generate and refine theories about how teachers are learning and how structure and culture affects them (Miles & Huberman, 1994). I also wrote memos to record and reflect upon my methodological decisions and personal reactions (Lincoln & Guba, 1985).

For data organization, I used NUD*IST, a qualitative software program, to organize and code textual data. Creating the codes and working with the texts helped me understand how the data could be "chunked," helped me to name those "chunks," and forced me to organize the data conceptually for the first time. Retrieving commonly coded interview quotes or field notes from the database helped me know whether I could substantiate the arguments that were emerging in my analytic memos. The codes also provided easy access to quotations I needed during the writing process. I feel it is important to note, however, that coding in itself does not lead a researcher to a powerful argument. It is merely a supportive tool for the intellect of the researcher.

I analyzed the teacher-level and contextual-level data separately and in combination, building theories about how one related to the other. To analyze each case, I wrote instrumental case studies drawn from my observational notes to characterize what the teacher's practice looked like, and how he or she used technology throughout the year. For each teacher, I produced a case study report (Yin, 1994) describing his or her teaching practice and history of professional learning.

I produced conceptual maps (Miles & Huberman, 1994) for each teacher's case study, describing relationships I saw between each teacher's learning and the school organization conceptual matrices to conduct a cross-case analysis of the relationship between organizational factors and teacher learning. These methods enabled me to explore the cultural supports that existed for all teachers, such as common educational goals, and those that existed only for some teachers, such as a departmental colleagues who frequently discussed technology use.

# References

Abelmann, C., Elmore, R., Even, J., Kenyon, S., & Marshall, J. (1999). *When accountability knocks, will anyone answer?* (Research Report No. RR-042). Philadelphia: Consortium for Policy, University of Pennyslvania, Graduate School of Education.

Anderson, J. R. (1985). *Cognitive psychology and its implications.* New York: W.H. Freeman.

Anderson, R. E., & Becker, H. J. (2001). *School investments in instructional technology* (TLC Report No. 8). Irvine: University of California, Center for Research on Information Technology and Organizations. Retrieved April 2, 2004, from http://www.crito.uci.edu/TLC/FINDINGS/report_8/REPORT_8.PDF

Ball, D. L., & Cohen, D. K. (1995). *Developing practice, developing practitioners: Toward a practice-based theory of professional education.* New York: National Commission on Teaching and America's Future.

Becker, H. J. (1994). *Analysis and trends of school use of new information technologies* (Contractor Report No. K3-0666.0). Washington, DC: U.S. Congress, Office of Technology Assessment.

Becker, H. J. (2000). Findings from the teaching, learning, and computing survey: Is Larry Cuban right? *Education Policy Analysis Archives, 8*(51). Retrieved March 31, 2004, from http://epaa.asu.edu/epaa/v8n51

Becker, H. J., Ravitz, J. L., & Wong, Y. (1999). *Teacher and teacher-directed student use of computers and software.* Irvine: University of California, Center for Research in Information Technology and Organizations. Retrieved March 31, 2004, from http://www.crito.uci.edu/tlc/findings/computeruse/

Becker, H. J., & Riel, M. M. (1999, September). *Teacher professionalism and the emergence of constructivist-compatible pedagogies.* Paper presented at the American Educational Research Association, Montreal, Canada. Retrieved March 31, 2004, from http://www.crito.uci.edu/tlc/findings/special_report2/index.htm

Bloom, B. S. (1956). *Taxonomy of educational objectives: The classification of educational goals, by a committee of college and university examiners.* New York: D. McKay.

Bogdan, R., & Biklen, S. K. (1982). *Qualitative research for education: An introduction to theory and methods.* Boston: Allyn and Bacon.

Bolman, L. G., & Deal, T. E. (1991). *Reframing organizations: Artistry, choice, and leadership.* San Francisco: Jossey-Bass.

Borko, H., & Putnam, R. T. (1996). Learning to teach. In D. C. Berliner & R. C. Calfee (Eds.), *Handbook of educational psychology* (pp. 673–708). New York: Simon and Schuster Macmillan.

Bransford, J. D., Brown, A. L., & Cocking, R. R. (Eds.). (1999). *How people learn: Brain, mind, experience, and school.* Washington, DC: National Academy Press.

Brown, J. S., & Duguid, P. (1989). Situated cognition and the culture of learning. *Educational Researcher, 18*(1), 32–42.

Bruner, J. (1966). *Toward a theory of instruction.* Cambridge, MA: Harvard University Press.

Calderhead, J. (1996). Teachers: Beliefs and knowledge. In D. C. Berliner & R. C. Calfee (Eds.), *Handbook of educational psychology* (pp. 709–725). New York: Simon and Schuster Macmillan.

Cinnamond, J. H., & Zimpher, N. L. (1990). Reflectivity as a function of community. In R. T. Clift, W. R. Houston, & M. C. Pugach (Eds.), *Encouraging reflective practice in education: An analysis of issues and programs* (pp. 57–72). New York: Teachers College Press.

Clark, C. M. (1986). Ten years of conceptual development in research on teacher thinking. In M. Ben-Peretz, R. Bromme, & R. Halkes (Eds.), *Advances of research on teacher thinking* (pp. 7–20). Lisse, Netherlands: Swets and Zeitlinger.

Cohen, D. K. (1987). Educational technology, policy, and practice. *Educational Evaluation and Policy Analysis, 9*(2), 153–170.

Cohen, D. K., McLaughlin, M. W., & Talbert, J. E. (Eds.). (1993). *Teaching for understanding: Challenges for policy and practice.* San Francisco: Jossey-Bass.

Cole, M., & Scribner, S. (1974). *Culture and thought: A psychological introduction.* New York: Wiley.

Collins, A. (1990). The role of computer technology in restructuring schools. In K. Sheingold & M. S. Tucker (Eds.), *Restructuring for learning with technology* (pp. 29–46). New York: Center for Technology in Education.

Cuban, L. (1986). *Teachers and machines: The classroom use of technology since 1920.* New York: Teachers College Press.

Cuban, L. (2001). *Oversold and underused: Computers in the classroom.* Cambridge, MA: Harvard University Press.

D'Andrade, R. (1995). *The development of cognitive anthropology.* New York: Cambridge University Press.

Darling-Hammond, L. (1995). Changing conceptions of teaching and teacher development. *Teacher Education Quarterly, 22*(4), 9–26.

Darling-Hammond, L. (1997a). *Doing what matters most: Investing in quality teaching.* New York: National Commission on Teaching and America's Future.

Darling-Hammond, L. (1997b). *The right to learn: A blueprint for creating schools that work.* San Francisco: Jossey-Bass.

Darling-Hammond, L., & McLaughlin, M. W. (1996). Policies that support professional development in an era of reform. In M. W. McLaughlin & I. Oberman (Eds.), *Teacher learning: New policies, new practices* (pp. 202–218). New York: Teachers College Press.

David, J. (1990). Restructuring and technology: Partners in change. In K. Sheingold & M. S. Tucker (Eds.), *Restructuring for learning with technology* (pp. 75–89). New York: Center for Technology in Education.

Deal, T. E., & Peterson, K. D. (1999). *Shaping school culture: The heart of leadership*. San Francisco: Jossey-Bass.

Dede, C. J. (1990). Imaging technology's role in restructuring for learning. In K. Sheingold & M. S. Tucker (Eds.), *Restructuring for learning with technology* (pp. 49–72). New York: Center for Technology in Education.

Duffy, T. M., & Jonassen, D. H. (1992). Constructivism: New implications for instructional technology. In T. M. Duffy & D. H. Jonassen (Eds.), *Constructivism and the technology of instruction: A conversation* (pp. 1–16). Hillsdale, NJ: Lawrence Erlbaum.

Elmore, R. F. (1995). Teaching, learning, and school organization: Principles of practice and the regularities of schooling. *Educational Administration Quarterly, 31*(3), 355–374.

Elmore, R. F., & Burney, D. (1997). *Investing in teacher learning: Staff development and instructional improvement in Community School District #2, New York City.* New York: National Commission on Teaching and America's Future.

Elmore, R. F., & McLaughlin, M. W. (1988). *Steady work: Policy, practice, and the reform of American education*. Santa Monica, CA: Rand.

Elmore, R. F., Peterson, P. L., & McCarthey, S. J. (1996). *Restructuring in the classroom: Teaching, learning and school organization*. San Francisco: Jossey-Bass.

Fullan, M. (1993). *Change forces: Probing the depths of educational reform*. Bristol, PA: Falmer Press.

Fullan, M. (1995). The school as a learning organization: Distant dreams. *Theory into Practice, 34*(4), 230–235.

Gardner, H. (1985). *The mind's new science: A history of the cognitive revolution*. New York: Basic Books.

Gardner, H. (1991). *The unschooled mind*. New York: Basic Books.

Geertz, C. (1973). Thick description: Toward an interpretive theory of culture. In *The interpretation of cultures* (pp. 3–30). New York: Basic Books.

Glaser, R. (1984). The role of knowledge. *American Psychologist, 39*(2), 93–104.

Glaser, B. G., & Strauss, A. L. (1967). *The discovery of grounded theory: Strategies for qualitative research*. New York: Aldine.

Glennan, T. K., & Melmed, A. (1996). *Fostering the use of educational technology: Elements of a national strategy*. Santa Monica, CA: RAND.

Goodlad, J. I. (1984). *A place called school: Prospects for the future*. New York: McGraw Hill.

Gordon, D. T. (Ed.). (2000). *The digital classroom: How technology is changing the way we teach and learn*. Cambridge, MA: Harvard Education Letter.

Grimmett, P. P., & Erickson, G. L. (Eds.). (1988). *Reflection in teacher education*. New York: Teachers College Press.

Grimmett, P. P., MacKinnon, A. M., Erickson, G. L., & Riecken, T. J. (1990). Reflective practice in teacher education. In R. T. Clift, R. W. Houston, & M. C. Pugach (Eds.), *Encouraging reflective practice in education: An analysis of issues and programs* (pp. 20–38). New York: Teachers College Press.

Grossman, P. L. (1990). *The making of a teacher: Teacher knowledge and teacher education*. New York: Teachers College Press.

Hall, G., & Hord, S. (1987). *Change in schools: Facilitating the process*. Albany, NY: State University of New York Press.

Hammersley, M., & Atkinson, P. (1995). *Ethnography: Principles in practice* (2nd ed.). New York: Routledge.

Hargreaves, A. (1993). Individualism and individuality: Interpreting teacher culture. In J. W. Little & M. W. McLaughlin (Eds.), *Teachers' work: Individuals, colleagues, and contexts* (pp. 51–76). New York: Teachers College Press.

Holmes, H. W. (1937). *Shall teachers be scholars?* (Occasional Paper). Cambridge, MA: Harvard University.

Honey, M., Culp, K. M., & Spielvogel, R. (1999). Critical issue: Using technology to improve student achievement. *Pathways to School Improvement*. Retrieved March 26, 2004, from http://www.ncrel.org/sdrs/areas/issues/methods/technlgy/te800.htm

Huberman, M. (1989). The professional life cycle of teachers. *Teachers College Record, 91*(1), 31–57.

Huberman, M. (1993). *The lives of teachers*. New York: Teachers College Press.

Huberman, M. A., & Miles, M. B. (1984). *Innovation up close: How school improvement works*. New York: Plenum Press.

Johnson, S. M. (1990). The primacy and potential of high school departments. In M. W. McLaughlin, J. E. Talbert, & N. Bascia (Eds.), *The contexts of teaching in secondary school: Teachers' realities* (pp. 167–184). New York: Teachers College Press.

Jonassen, D. H. (1996). *Computers in the classroom: Mindtools for critical thinking*. Englewood Cliffs, NJ: Prentice-Hall.

Lampert, M. (1993). Teachers' thinking about students' thinking about geometry: The effects of new teaching tools. In J. L. Schwartz, M. Yerushalmy, & B. Wilson (Eds.), *The geometric supposer: What is it a case of?* (pp. 143–178). Hillsdale, NJ: Lawrence Erlbaum.

LeBaron, J. F., & Collier, C. (Eds.). (2001). *Technology in its place: Successful technology infusion in schools*. San Francisco: Jossey-Bass.

Lieberman, A. (Ed.). (1988). *Building a professional culture in schools*. New York: Teachers College Press.

Lieberman, A. (1996). Practices that support teacher development: Transforming conceptions of professional learning. In M. W. McLaughlin & I. Oberman (Eds.), *Teacher learning: New policies, new practices* (pp. 185–201). New York: Teachers College Press.

Lincoln, Y., & Guba, E. (1985). *Naturalistic inquiry*. Beverly Hills, CA: Sage.

Little, J. W. (1981, April). *The power of organizational setting: School norms and staff development*. Paper presented at the annual meeting of the American Educational Research Association, Los Angeles, CA.

Little, J. W. (1982). Norms of collegiality and experimentation: Workplace conditions of school success. *American Educational Research Journal, 19*(3), 325–340.

Little, J. W. (1993). Teachers' professional development in a climate of educational reform. *Educational Evaluation and Policy Analysis, 15*(2), 129–151.

Little, J. W., & McLaughlin, M. W. (1993). *Teachers' work: Individuals, colleagues, and contexts.* New York: Teachers College Press.

Lortie, D. C. (1975). *Schoolteacher: A sociological study.* Chicago: University of Chicago Press.

Martin, J. (1992). *Cultures in organizations: Three perspectives.* New York: Oxford University Press.

McLaughlin, M. W., & Oberman, I. (Eds.). (1996). *Teacher learning: New policies, new practices.* New York: Teachers College Press.

McLaughlin, M. W., Talbert, J. E., & Bascia, N. (Eds.). (1990). *The contexts of teaching in secondary schools: Teachers' realities.* New York: Teachers College Press.

Means, B. (Ed.). (1991). *Technology and education reform.* San Francisco: Jossey-Bass.

Means, B., & Olson, K. (1995). *Technology's role in educational reform: Findings from a national study of innovating schools.* Menlo Park, CA: SRI International.

Means, B., Penuel, W. R., & Padilla, C. (2001). *The connected school: Technology and learning in high school.* San Francisco: Jossey-Bass.

Miles, M., & Huberman, M. (1994). *Qualitative data analysis.* Thousand Oaks, CA: Sage.

Mintzberg, H. (1979). *The structuring of organizations.* Englewood Cliffs, NJ: Prentice-Hall.

Morgan, G. (1997). *Images of organization* (2nd ed.). Thousand Oaks, CA: Sage.

Nelson, B. S., & Hammerman, J. K. (1996). Reconceptualizing teaching: Moving toward the creation of intellectual communities of students, teachers, and teacher educators. In M. W. McLaughlin & I. Oberman (Eds.), *Teacher learning: New policies, new practices* (pp. 3–21). New York: Teachers College Press.

Newman, D. (1991). *Technology as support for school structure and school restructuring* (Technical Report No. 14). New York: Bank Street Center for Technology in Education.

Newmann, F. M., & Wehlage, G. G. (1995). *Successful school restructuring.* Madison: University of Wisconsin, Center on Organization and Restructuring of Schools.

Olson, D. R., & Bruner, J. S. (1996). Folk psychology and folk pedagogy. In D. R. Olson & N. Torrance (Eds.), *The handbook of education and human development: New models of learning, teaching and schooling* (pp. 9–27). Cambridge, MA: Blackwell.

Papert, S. (1980). *Mindstorms: Children, computers, and powerful ideas.* New York: Basic Books.

Patton, M. Q. (1990). *Qualitative evaluation and research methods* (2nd ed.). Thousand Oaks, CA: Sage.

Perkins, D. N., Schwartz, J. L., West, M. M., & Wiske, M. S. (Eds.). (1995). *Software goes to school: Teaching for understanding with new technologies.* New York: Oxford University Press.

Peters, T. (1988). *Thriving on chaos: Handbook for a management revolution.* New York: HarperCollins.

Peters, T., & Waterman, R. H. (1988). *In search of excellence.* New York: HarperCollins.

Pope, M. (1993). Anticipating teacher thinking. In C. Day, J. Calderhead, & P. Denicolo (Eds.), *Research on teacher thinking: Understanding professional development* (pp. 19–33). Bristol, PA: Falmer Press.

Pope, M. L., & Denicolo, P. (1986). Intuitive theories—A researcher's dilemma. *British Educational Journal, 12*(2), 153–165.

Powell, A. G., Farrar, E., & Cohen, D. K. (1985). *The shopping mall high school: Winners and losers in the educational marketplace.* Boston, MA: Houghton Mifflin.

Resnick, L. (1987). *Education and learning to think.* Washington, DC: National Academy Press.

Rogers, E. M. (1995). *Diffusion of innovations* (4th ed.). New York: Free Press.

Rosenholtz, S. J. (1991). *Teachers' workplace: The social organization of schools.* New York: Teachers College Press.

Rossi, I., & O'Higgins, E. (1980). The development of theories of culture. In I. Rossi (Ed.), *People in culture* (pp. 31–78). New York: Praeger.

Sandholtz, J. H., Ringstaff, C., & Dwyer, D. C. (1997). *Teaching with technology: Creating student-centered classrooms.* New York: Teachers College Press.

Sarason, S. (1990). *The predictable failure of educational reform.* San Francisco: Jossey-Bass.

Sarason, S. (1996). *Revisiting "The culture of the school and the problem of change."* New York: Teachers College Press.

Scardamalia, M., Bereiter, C., Brett, C., Burtis, P. J., Calhoun, C., & Lea, N. (1992). Educational applications of a networked communal database. *Interactive Learning Environments, 2*(1), 45–71.

Scardamalia, M., Bereiter, C., & Lamon, M. (1994). The CSILE Project: Trying to bring the classroom into World 3. In K. McGilly (Ed.), *Classroom lessons: Integrating cognitive theory and classroom practice* (pp. 201–228). Cambridge, MA: MIT Press.

Scardamalia, M., Bereiter, C., McLean, R. S., Swallow, J., & Woodruff, E. (1991–92). Computer-supported intentional learning environments. *Journal of Educational Computing Research, 5*(1), 51–68.

Schein, E. H. (1992). *Organizational culture and leadership.* San Francisco: Jossey-Bass.

Schön, D. A. (1983). *The reflective practitioner: How professionals think in action.* New York: Basic Books.

Schön, D. A. (1987). *Educating the reflective practitioner: Toward a new design for teaching and learning in the professions.* San Francisco: Jossey-Bass.

Schön, D. A. (1988). Coaching reflective teaching. In P. P. Grimmett & G. L. Erickson (Eds.), *Reflection in teacher education* (pp. 19–30). New York: Teachers College Press.

Schwartz, J. L. (1995). Shuttling between the particular and the general: Reflections on the role of conjecture and hypothesis in the generation of knowledge in science and mathematics. In D. N. Perkins, J. L. Schwartz, M. M.

West, & M. S. Wiske (Eds.), *Software goes to school: Teaching for understanding with new technologies* (pp. 93–105). New York: Oxford University Press.

Scott, W. R., & Cohen, R. C. (1995). Work units in organizations: Ransacking the literature. In L. S. Siskin & J. W. Little (Eds.), *The subjects in question: Departmental organization and the high school* (pp. 48–67). New York: Teachers College Press.

Scribner, S. (1986). Thinking in action: Some characteristics of practical thought. In R. J. Sternberg & R. K. Wagner (Eds.), *Practical intelligence: Nature and origins of competence in the everyday world* (pp. 13–30). New York: Cambridge University Press.

Senge, P. M. (1990). *The fifth discipline: The art and practice of the learning organization.* New York: Doubleday/Currency.

Sergiovanni, T. (2000). *The lifeworld of leadership.* San Francisco: Jossey-Bass.

Sheingold, K. (1990). Restructuring for learning with technology: The potential for synergy. In K. Sheingold & M. S. Tucker (Eds.), *Restructuring for learning with technology* (pp. 9–27). New York: Center for Technology in Education.

Sheingold, K., & Tucker, M. S. (Eds.). (1990). *Restructuring for learning with technology.* New York: Center for Technology in Education.

Shulman, L. S. (1986). Those who understand: Knowledge growth in teaching. *Educational Researcher, 15*(2), 4–14.

Shulman, L. S. (1987). Knowledge and teaching: Foundations of the new reform. *Harvard Educational Review, 57*(1), 1–22.

Siskin, L. S. (1994). *Realms of knowledge: Academic departments in secondary schools.* London: Falmer Press.

Siskin, L. S., & Little, J. W. (Eds.). (1995). *The subjects in question: Departmental organization and the high school.* New York: Teachers College Press.

Sizer, T. R. (1985). *Horace's compromise: The dilemma of the American high school.* Boston: Houghton Mifflin.

Smircich, L. (1983). Concepts of culture and organizational analysis. *Administrative Science Quarterly, 28*(3), 339–358.

Snyder, T., & Palmer, J. (1986). *In search of the most amazing thing: Children, education, and computers.* Reading, MA: Addison-Wesley.

Sokoloff, D. R., Thornton, R., & Laws, P. (1999). *RealTime physics.* Hoboken, NJ: Wiley.

Spillane, J. P., & Jennings, N. E. (1995, April). *Constructing a challenging pedagogy for all students: Contrasting the rhetoric of reform with practice and the rehetoric of practitioners.* Paper presented at the meeting of the American Educational Research Association, New York, NY.

Stake, R. E. (1995). *The art of case study research.* Thousand Oaks, CA: Sage.

State of the union: Clinton outlines his vision for nation's transition to the 21st century. (1999, January 20). *New York Times,* p. A22.

Swidler, A. (2001). *Talk of love: How culture matters.* Chicago: University of Chicago Press.

Talbert, J. (1995). Boundaries of teachers' professional communities in U.S. high schools: Power and precariousness of the subject department. In L. S. Siskin & J. W. Little (Eds.), *The subjects in question: Departmental organization and the high school* (pp. 68–94). New York: Teachers College Press.

Trumbull, D. (1989). Computer-generated challenges to school culture: One teacher's story. *Journal of Curriculum Studies, 21*(5), 457–469.

Tufts University. (2003). Perseus Digital Library. Retrieved March 31, 2004, from http://www.perseus.tufts.edu

Tyack, D., & Cuban, L. (1997). *Tinkering toward utopia: A century of public school reform.* Cambridge, MA: Harvard University Press.

University of Toronto. (2003). *Institute for Knowledge Innovation and Technology.* Retrieved March 31, 2004, from http://www.ikit.org/

U.S. Bureau of the Census. (2000). U.S. Census, 2000. Retrieved from http://www.census.gov/main/www/cen2000.html

U. S. Bureau of the Census. (2002). *Statistical abstract of the U.S.: 2001. Computers for student instruction in elementary and secondary schools: 2000–2001.* Washington, D.C.: Congressional Information Service.

U.S. Congress, Office of Technology Assessment. (1988). *Power On! New tools for teaching and learning.* Retrieved April 2, 2004, from http://www.wws.princeton.edu/cgi-bin/byteserv.prl/~ota/disk2/1988/8831/8831.PDF

U.S. Congress, Office of Technology Assessment. (1995). *Teachers and technology: Making the connection.* Retrieved April 2, 2004, from http://www.wws.princeton.edu/cgi-bin/byteserv.prl/~ota/disk1/1995/9541.PDF

U.S. Department of Education. (2004). *National education technology plan.* Retrieved April 2, 2004, from http://www.nationaledtechplan.org/

Vernier, D. (2004). *Vernier software and technology.* Retrieved March 31, 2004, http://www.vernier.com/

Weick, K. E. (1995). *Sensemaking in organizations.* Thousand Oaks, CA: Sage.

Wenglinsky, H. (1998). *Does it compute? The relationship between educational technology and student achievement in mathematics* (Report No. ED425 191). Princeton, NJ: Educational Testing Service.

Westheimer, J. (1998). *Among schoolteachers: Community, autonomy and ideology in teachers' work.* New York: Teachers College Press.

Wiske, M. S. (Ed.). (1998). *Teaching for understanding: A practical framework.* San Francisco: Jossey-Bass.

Wiske, M. S., & Houde, R. (1993). From recitation to construction: Teachers change with new technologies. In J. L. Schwartz, M. Yerushalmy, & B. Wilson (Eds.), *The geometric supposer: What is it a case of?* (pp. 193–216). Hillsdale, NJ: Lawrence Erlbaum.

Wiske, M. S., Niguidula, D., & Shepard, J. W. (1988). *Collaborative research goes to school: Guided inquiry with computers in classrooms* (Technical Report No. TR88-3). Cambridge, MA: Harvard Graduate School of Education, Educational Technology Center.

Yin, R. K. (1994). *Case study research: Design and methods* (2nd ed.). Thousand Oaks, CA: Sage.

# Index

# About the Author

EILEEN COPPOLA is a researcher in the Center for Education and lecturer in the Department of Education at Rice University. She received her EdD from Harvard Graduate School of Education in 2000 in the area of Administration, Policy, and Social Planning, with a focus on Urban Superintendency. She previously completed an MA at Teachers College, Columbia University, in Instructional Technology and Media, and has worked in public school systems in New York City, Philadelphia, Boston, and Houston. Her research addresses the complex relationships among policy, organization, culture, and schooling, and she is committed to the improvement of public schools, especially in urban areas.